# Searching for Home

## A World War II Orphan's True Story
## of Survival and Grace

The Lifetime Memories of
Inna Wolkovich Gardner Nichols
as Told to and Written by

## Alice Frick Hagaman

ISBN 978-1-64416-592-8 (paperback)
ISBN 978-1-64515-941-4 (hardcover)
ISBN 978-1-64416-593-5 (digital)

Christian Faith Publishing, Inc.
832 Park Avenue
Meadville, PA 16335
www.christianfaithpublishing.com

Printed in the United States of America

For Inna's grandchildren
Aaron James Nichols
Justin Michael Nichols
and their future generations

# Acknowledgments

From the first day when Inna and I met for lunch to plan how I might write about her lifetime memories, the friendly staff at the Roxboro Road, Durham, Chick-fil-A expressed their hospitality and interest in Inna's story. During our weekly visits, they cordially offered a quiet booth (with an electrical outlet for my computer) for us to enjoy eating our meal while discussing Inna's past experiences. We stayed for hours! Special thanks to Matt Rice and Austin Franks for featuring our visits via videos on their Chick-fil-A website. "It's my pleasure!"

I especially thank Robert L. Wallace, our former pastor, for his generous time reading and editing some of my early drafts. His comments, such as, *"I can hear Inna speaking through your words,"* and *"You truly have captured her spirit and courage,"* gave me confidence that I could reflect Inna's character and faith in my writing.

My niece, Meredith Steadman, a high school World History teacher in Chesapeake, Virginia, immediately showed interest in Inna's story from a historical perspective. It was very helpful when she read some of my drafts to verify the historical accuracy of dates and happenings that Inna described in her experiences. Meredith valued Inna's accounts and recognized how readers young and old might gain sensitivity for others who have endured the effects of war, destruction, and loss. She valued some of the challenges that Inna had as a war refugee and as a Non-English speaking immigrant in a new country;

situations that she felt some of her students could relate to in their own lives.

I am forever thankful to my husband, John, for his endearing patience and support to make this book possible. His comments as he read my work helped me find clarity and attention to important details in my writing.

I especially cherish the times I have with my daughter, Amy, who shares her faith with me. After reading one of my manuscript drafts while on a mother-daughter trip, Amy encouraged me to include biblical scriptures that relate to the events in Inna's story. I believe her witness to me empowered Inna's story.

I appreciate Inna's husband, Graham Nichols, and their son, Ernest, for the support and encouragement they gave to Inna throughout our writing process. They cherish the powerful impact her lifetime memories will have for their family's future generations.

Inna and I express sincere appreciation to the faithful members of Aldersgate United Methodist Church in Durham, North Carolina, and our pastor, Dr. Bryan Faggart, for their loving expressions of kindness, friendship, and encouragement supporting the writing of our book. Their actions gently reminded us to "Do all the good you can…as long as ever you can," as quoted from John Wesley.

Last but certainly not least, I express my heartfelt appreciation and love to Inna. I thank her for sharing her most personal thoughts and reflections of lifetime memories. There were times when we laughed, cried, and prayed as Inna related her past experiences. She is a mighty witness to her faith and an enduring inspiration to me.

# Preface

## Where is God in All of This?

It was a brisk and sunny Sunday morning in February, 2014, as I was sitting in the church sanctuary waiting for my "pew buddy," Inna Nichols, to arrive for the eleven o'clock morning worship service. As I began my personal meditation, my thoughts and prayers for peace focused on the recent international events that had dominated the past week's media news reports regarding the suffering of the Ukrainian people in Crimea who were under siege from recent Russian invasions. The grim pictures on the television and stories from local and international news correspondents presented the horrific plights of hundreds or thousands of displaced refugees as a result of Vladimir Putin's determination to occupy Crimea. The world was shocked by this seemingly unprovoked aggression, and to me, it all seemed to be such a tragic mess. As I sat there, I asked myself, *Where is God in all of this?*

Knowing that Inna was from the Ukraine area, I turned to greet her and quietly asked what thoughts she might have regarding these recent events. Her response was abrupt, "Russia has wanted to claim the Ukraine as part of Russia ever since the tenth century—this is nothing new!"

I then asked, "Do you have *any* family left in that area?"

She shook her head, "No—I have no family—when I was a very young child, I lost *all* of my family members during Josef

Stalin's regime." She paused and her voice began to drop off, "I have such a story to tell about my life… I so much want my grandsons, Aaron and Justin, to know about me and where I came from. They really know nothing about me—only that I am their grandmother who speaks with a *funny* accent." Showing me her swollen and knurled hands, she said, "I cannot *write!*"

Looking into Inna's teary eyes, I immediately responded to her without thinking, "I will write your story if you will tell it to me!"

Inna immediately took my hand into hers and nodded with a grateful smile, "Thank you, thank you!"

For a moment, everything seemed to be a blur for me as the organ music started playing, and the congregation began singing the first hymn. My immediate thoughts were, *Oh God, what was I thinking, what have I done—what have I promised?* I must admit that I do not remember much about the pastor's message that morning as I was bargaining with God about how I did not have time to write this woman's story; my husband John and I were planning some retirement trips, and I was also continuing some part-time work with teachers in our school district. My calendar was too full already. And God, I just do not have a talent for writing! I asked his forgiveness for me making such a bold claim to Inna, and surely as my friend, she would understand that I could not carry out her wishes.

As I continued to struggle with my agreement to Inna to write her story, I rationalized to myself, Inna is eighty years old, and she will just share with me a few of her memories—that's all. I will write her little stories down and make a paper cover so that she could give each of her grandsons a small booklet as a gift the next time she saw them. That's it! I will be done, and I will have fulfilled my promise to her! This won't be hard! By the end of the worship service, my spirit felt greatly relieved as

I thought *God and I* had a plan, and I was sure He would be pleased with my commitment to help my dear friend. I did not realize that God had a plan for me that was far better than my own.

The following Friday, a usual cold winter day, Inna and I met for lunch over some hot Chick-fil-A chicken soup (comfort food) to talk about "her little stories" and how we might get started. Immediately, I was captivated—in awe of Inna's ability to remember her past—as she began to tell me about her childhood years during World War II. She shared with me her earliest memories with great details and emotion. It was very evident that Inna indeed had a compelling story to tell—many stories! Thus, we began our work together—me, the writer and Inna, the storyteller.

I realized Inna's stories are not "little," as they are very powerful and real memories of survival. I felt her passion, and eagerly looked forward to the stories she would share with me each time we met. During our writing sessions, I typed (hunt and pecked) her memories as she told them to me. She gave me the "happenings," and I did the wordsmithing, adding descriptions and elaborations. I quickly learned that her story did not require my "writing talent," as the story spoke for itself. There were many times when we prayed, cried, and laughed together as she shared the details of her experiences. When Inna became immersed in describing her past life events, I often probed her with many questions to better understand her true feelings and reflections. Thus, when I returned to my computer at home to work on my writing, I truly felt that she was beside me (and so was God).

When Inna and I were together, we frequently talked about how God and the Holy Scriptures were speaking through her life experiences. I repeatedly asked Inna, as I so often asked myself when I was writing, "Where was God in all of this?" Now, after completing Inna's story five years later, it is up to you, the reader, to answer that question.

> *The aged women…shall teach the younger women…(Titus 2:4, NIV)*

# Introduction

This story must be taken in the context of its time. Germany was defeated in World War I (1914–1918), and its people were still suffering from the ravages of war. The peace settlements were vindictive toward Germany and its allies. The terms of the 1919 Treaty of Versailles harshly condemned Germany for the devastation of the war and demanded reparations. The world was experiencing an economic crisis of the 1930s that totally debilitated growth and prosperity. All of Europe was feeling the tensions of the establishment of new governments, social classes, and political movements such as Fascism and Communism.

Specific to Germany, Adolf Hitler was rising through the political ranks establishing the Nazi Party and trying to restore Germany to its prominent place among the nations. His ultimate plan was to make the Arian race supreme and lead the world and to establish German military control of Europe and beyond. Amid the social unrest and political turmoil, fragile alliances began to be created among Germany, Italy, Spain, and Japan; as well as the Allied forces of France, Great Britain, the Soviet Union, and the United States. The world's political and social climate was fragile and very unstable. The world was again at war.

Inna Wolkovich Gardner Nichols's story is not a recount of the horrors of war, for those stories have already been written. Her story is a true personal recollection based on her memories as a young orphan girl caught up in the ravages and consequences of war as so many thousands experienced. It has been claimed that the primary victims of any war are the children. Inna was one of those children. What is written by the author is primarily based on Inna's personal memories. At this point in her life of eighty plus years, the events described in this story stand out clearly in her mind.

> *These things I remember as I pour out my soul… with shouts of joy and thanksgiving…(Psalm 42:4, NIV)*

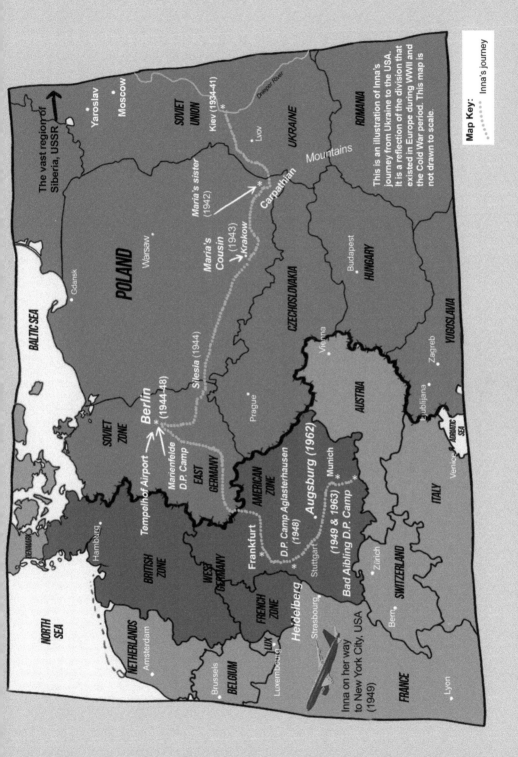

**Map Key:**
············ Inna's journey

# In the Beginning

I was born in Kharkiv (eastern Ukraine) on August 11, 1933, to Ninna Fidler and Anatolii Sergeevich Wolkovich. My parents were already experiencing the consequences of the political and economic unrest of the time. In my birth year, Adolf Hitler became the Chancellor of Germany strengthening his plan to create a one-party Nazi nation. By the time I was one year old, Hitler had emerged as the Fuhrer and was the supreme dictator. Premier Josef Stalin was also gaining oppressive power as dictator of the Soviet Union.

My mother came from a wealthy German-Jewish merchant family living in Kiev, the capital city of Ukraine. During the time of the Russian Czars, they had a large home and estate built on a cliff above the Dnieper River. Around 1918, the year that World War I ended and long before my mother met my father, Ninna married a man (name unknown) who lived and worked in Kharkov. I really know nothing of my mother's first marriage other than she had a daughter, Magdelena "Dalia" born around 1919.

My mother was a highly educated woman, earning a gold diploma from the gymnasium, a school much like a community college. For a woman of her time and place, this was a high accomplishment. However, none of her education was of any value during the Communist regime under Stalin. She was not a member of the Communist "classless society." Therefore, her once fine home was later seized by the Soviet government and turned into small apartments of which she was then forced into a caretaker role of cleaning and maintaining the property.

My father was a Russian born in Yaroslavl, a town southeast of Moscow. He was a writer and poet, an ardent Leninist, and a member of the Communist Party. It is interesting for me to think about why he married my mother. They each had such different values and beliefs. Was it love, or did my father pity my mother's circumstances? She did not fit into the new Communist society or so called—workers' paradise. The political philosophy of thought was contrary to her background of accumulated family wealth and tradition.

As a small child, I remember my father as a tall man with dark curly hair and gentle hands. He was loving in every way as he showed great concern and care for me. My earliest memory, about the age of three, was going with my parents to the eastern shore of the Dnieper River where there was a beach to bathe and enjoy the cool water. While there, I remember a wall of water or a wave causing me to go under the water and my father rescuing me. How safe and secure I felt in his arms! At that time, we lived about five miles from Kiev, and I vividly recall walking home with my parents late one evening. My father picked me up in his arms, for I must have gotten tired. As he held me close, I looked up at the moon, and it seemed to me to look like an evil man grinning down on us. I buried my face in my father's shoulder, and again I felt safe and protected.

Around 1936, during a time when Stalin sent thousands to the harsh frigid work camps of Siberia for the least charges, my father was given a ten-year sentence. He was denounced as a Bolshevik Lenin supporter and accused by his best friend and fellow writer. Was it professional jealousy, or because he had married my mother, a daughter from a wealthy family and therefore, an enemy of the state? In those days, it was easy to get rid of your rivals.

The Soviet government kept all its citizens under vigilant surveillance. It was difficult for persons to go into hiding and not be found. As people moved from place to place, they were required to register with the Soviet authorities. Of course, most people did not daily travel more than eight or ten miles from their homes. There was little trust among neighbors because people, out of their own desperation, were known to report any suspicious activities among their "friends." As Stalin gained more authority and power over the Russian people, his ruthless plan to purge the leaders and supporters of the Bolshevik Comrades by sentencing them to exile or death had a tragic impact on my young life.

My last and most haunting memory of my father was when he was in a Kiev prison awaiting his transfer to Siberia. I remember him holding me on his lap while stroking my small hands, saying sadly, "Who will cut your fingernails now?" What a strange thing to say…but now as I reflect on this painful time, I am comforted that my father was so concerned for my smallest need and grieved that he would not be there for me.

My mother, then pregnant with another child, was left in a desperate situation to take care of two very young children. How distressful it must have been for my father to realize that he would never see his youngest baby born after he was taken away.

The many Siberian work camps were brutal, and people did not survive for more than four or five years. I can only imagine the horrific conditions that my father must have endured. The bitter cold and starvation, not to mention the harsh treatment inflicted upon him by the prison guards, must have nearly sent my father out of his mind. I am sure that he thought daily of my mother and his two young children he left behind. What grief it must have been for him to bear knowing that his family of an exiled "enemy of the state" sent to Siberia would certainly feel repercussions. My mother and her children were deemed as outcasts from Soviet society.

I, too, grieved. As a very young child, it was hard for me to understand why my father was no longer in my life. I never saw him again. My young mind could not grasp why he was gone. Where was he? Where did he go? Over time, I realized that my world would be without him. This first tragedy taught me to accept life as it came to me; Russian children just *live life as it is*!

My mother, facing her world without my father, grieved for him and her past life style of wealth and prosperity. Under Stalin's regime, she was a "worker of the state," only a servant laboring in the apartments controlled by the government— property that once belonged to her family's estate.

I have a few early childhood memories of my Uncle Yuriy who was my mother's brother, and her two elderly aunts who all lived in one of the small cramped bedroom apartments. I remember my mother's former large house permeated with the smell of food simmering in pots on hotplates outside each apartment door. As I think back to that time, I cannot recall observing the preparation of food in the kitchen. It seems strange to me that food was only available to the tenants outside their apartment doors in the dimly lit hallways for them to eat any time during the day and evening.

I also recall taking walks in the former garden areas of the estate with my mother and my seventeen-year-old half-sister, Dalia, who was no longer living with us as she was a ward of the state. Since she was not my father's birth child, she was accepted by the Communist Party and became a Komsomol (*Komunisticheskaya Sovietskaya Molodost*), a young person of the

Communist Youth Movement. I have only small recollections of her being present in my young life.

I remember that we could see beautiful views of the Dnieper River from the high cliffs of the property. This river is the life blood of the Ukraine, and it lives in many songs, poetry, stories, and the history of its people. The entire estate grounds had lost their grandeur. I am sure my mother must have missed seeing the beautifully manicured gardens during the time of her youth. As a child, I remember thinking how odd the barren dead trees appeared as the tree limbs were cut for firewood, only the stumps were left. As I think back to my memories of the dried out and broken garden, I cannot help to think that it resembled my family. We, too, had lost so much, and we were just remnants of what we used to be—a bygone era.

My mother, pregnant with my younger sister, Alya, and so devastated over the imprisonment of my father and the loss of her family's home and former life, became absorbed in her own grief. She was so overwhelmed and suffering from depression; she found it impossible to care for me. Out of her desperation, she asked Maria Afanasiev, a friend of her mother's mother (a grandmother I never knew), to take me into her home outside of Kiev where she lived with her second husband, Artemiy Vasilevich. Maria's first husband had died in 1918, and not long after, Maria experienced the heartbreaking death of her nine-year-old daughter. Perhaps Maria agreed to take care of me because she understood my need for motherly care, and *her* need to love a child again. This critical decision for my mother to give me to Maria created unimaginable future events.

*Though my father and mother forsake me, the LORD will receive me. (Psalm 27:10, NIV)*

# Going Forward

Around 1938, life with Maria and Artemiy was not bad as Artemiy had a job working in construction helping to build a new town west of Kiev. Russia was trying to rebuild the economy and provide labor jobs for its people. Perhaps it was Artemiy's construction job that made it possible for us to live in one of the rooms for "workers of the state." We lived from day to day, thinking life would be good for all in the future. Hope was still alive for social justice and prosperity.

As a five-year-old child, I remember one evening when we attended a private celebration in the new town to commemorate Lenin's birthday. At the party, the workers had me stand on a table and asked me to recite a beautiful poem written by my father. He must have written this poem during his early years as he lauded the plans Lenin had for a new and better Russia and its people. I only recall a few phrases…

> Shall we erect a monument to him [Lenin]?
> No, his worthy monument is labor,
> He wants to fill the Volga
> With the horns of a thousand ships.

In this poem, my father is expressing that Lenin wanted the great Volga River to be filled with a thousand ships of commerce. He wanted prosperity to come to the Russian people—to work for the good of all! There was to be no hierarchy of classes—

only one mighty Russian society—as envisioned by Lenin! My father was a dreamer and visionary for a better Russian society, and he paid the heavy price for his outspoken ideas.

During this turbulent time in Russian history when life for common citizens was an undue hardship, their spirit and vitality were evident. The Russians are resilient and proud people. I remember the rolling hills and the very cold winters of my motherland. We always had a lot of snow and ice that presented challenges in our small apartment which provided warmth and heat. Despite the bitter cold, I recall seeing people skiing on the hillsides outside of Kiev and enjoying their winter activities. The Russian people love their winter sports! As I think back to those early memories, I reflect on how people seem to find pleasure in small things that give them comfort.

One such memory was of a woman who lived in a tiny one room dwelling near us. She had a living fir tree (about as tall as I was at the time) that she had brought into her tiny living space. As a five-year-old child, I thought, how strange! I recall her telling me that she loved the smell of the pine tree. She kept the tree in her small room all year round and cared for it daily. I now wonder if that tree, a gift of Nature, was what gave her purpose and resolve to find a pleasing aspect in her life. She must have been very lonely and needed something "alive" to reassure her that life is precious. Therefore, she watered it, pruned it, and in return that tree gave her the comfort of its smell. I have often had this flashback of that woman with her tree wondering if she ever decorated it or hung any decorations on its branches… I guess that would be unlikely since the Russian government did not allow such activities related to religious celebrations, such as Christmas… I think she simply enjoyed the *scent* of a *living* thing.

The following year in 1939 Artemiy finished his construction work, and we moved closer to Kiev. Our lives soon became progressively worse. The Stalin regime was ruthless in how people were treated. We were no longer "willing workers of the state" but a low forced working class. We moved into a barrack-like structure where we were once again allotted one room for the three of us—Maria, Artemiy, and me. At that, we were lucky! Our living conditions were crowded and unsanitary, to say the least. We were living among a group of very uneducated people whom we had little contact with. This was because every day, except on Sunday, Maria and I walked the four miles through rain and snow to the outskirts of Kiev for Maria to go to work as a physician's assistant and for me to attend a local preschool. I remember that Maria wore a very thin coat, and I can only imagine now how cold she must have felt on our long walks during the winter months.

I have a haunting memory of seeing an old woman on one of the streets in Kiev as Maria and I passed her along our way. From a distance, it seemed to me that she was a beautiful lady wearing a fine black dress with lace on her collar, her cuffs, and inlaid lace on the bodice of her dress. However, as we walked closer, I could see that her once fine dress was dirty, shabby, and torn. She was asking people passing by if they could spare her a few rubles. As we approached her sitting on the street curb, I asked the woman in my childish way, why she was begging for money. I was perplexed as I thought that a lady wearing such a once fine dress could be so destitute. I will never forget her response with the sound she made from her weather-dried lips. The sound was something between a laugh and a sob. This memory will always stay with me. I do not recall ever seeing that poor woman again. Begging on the street was not allowed during the Soviet regime as such behavior would admit a failure of the Communist system.

Maria, now my guardian, had listed me as her dependent. Therefore, she was able to enroll me in one of the state-run preschools. I recall one time when I told one of the preschool workers that I had to leave early that day because my mother was going to pick me up. The worker immediately responded to my comment and gruffly shook her finger in my face, *"But you don't have a mother!"* What a crushing thing to say to a young child who was searching for a motherly bond. I remember this cruel event with great sorrow. It was a piercing feeling that I will never forget. The harsh reality of the loss of my mother was devastating even though Maria did all she could to fill the void.

It was extremely difficult living in our one room; sleeping, cooking, and eating in a terribly cramped space. An odd memory that I have of that drab room was when Artemiy told me that he wished that I could have piano lessons. This was the first time that I can recall someone expressing a "dream" for me. I thought, How preposterous! There was *no space* for a piano! As I think back to that time, I now realize that Artemiy's wish for me to know how to play the piano must have come from his sincere concern for me to have better opportunities in life. He must have thought that I was *worthy*!

Outside the doors of the individual rooms where multiple family members lived, there was a long hallway that led to the outside. Across the yard was a large wall that divided the living areas from the storage sheds. It is interesting to me now to think of what was in those storage places. Many of the sheds had been abandoned by families who had fled Kiev when the Germans took over the city. While Maria and Artemiy did not have a storage shed, there were others who had brought what little they had with them when they fled their previous homes.

I still wonder why these people felt that they needed to keep objects that they could not use at the time. The residents had so little to store! What could they possibly have of any value? I now think that people who have lost so much but still hold on to material belongings such as unusable furniture and "family treasures" want to have these items to remind them of their past memories and their hope for a better life in the future. How many times do I think, "I must keep this, for I might need it someday!" The destruction of war destroyed the hopes of so many people for a "someday."

My memory of this storage area goes on to recall that the toilet was just next to the storage sheds. As a child this "facility" was nothing new to me. Going to relieve myself was by today's standards deplorable! However, as bad and unpleasant as this experience was, it did provide wonderful results, for when I walked from the storage sheds past the "outhouse," I do remember there was a large community garden very close by that was full of delicious vegetables! Apparently the soil was *very well enriched*!

It is interesting to realize that even though there were many people who had to live in these cramped units of space where one might think that they would be friendly and connect with each other, the reality was that the people seemed to pull away from one another. There were so many persons crowded together, yet each one was so isolated! Perhaps this social structure created a tension among everyone because of their fear. Our neighbors stayed away from us, and we stayed away from them. No one trusted anyone! When I think on this, it is interesting to me to think how people can react to fear—rather than seeking each other for support—they may often pull into their own world so unlike the Russian people as a whole who are basically friendly people, full of character.

My memory takes me to a disturbing incident that reflects how cruel and spiteful people can be to each other as they are dealing with their own problems and pain. It happened one day when I was playing in a small courtyard area with some of the neighboring children. A group of women were standing close by and gossiping which was a common activity among the adults. Being curious, I wanted to listen to what they were saying. Among them was a woman from the Don River area where the people were known to be very fierce and combative. Her young daughter, about the age of three years old, was playing nearby. She had a switch in her hand and perhaps thinking she might get her mother's attention; she began to playfully switch me on my legs and arms not realizing that she was hurting me. As I immediately began to cry out, the women in the circle began to laugh which encouraged the little girl to continue hitting me more. Feeling attacked, I ran away. It was hard for me to understand why this mother did not stop her child's aggressive behavior toward me. Was it possible that these women could not feel empathy and see another child's physical pain? I have often wondered about how people can be so desensitized to the point that they ignore and even enjoy another's suffering. I immediately sought Maria's protection and avoided contact with this group of women, for I knew I could not trust them to keep me safe. It is interesting how young children learn very quickly who will protect them and who will not.

I recall the last time I saw my older half-sister, Dalia. It was in the later months of 1939 when she brought us candy, and called Alya and me her *"sestruschki"* (her dear little sisters). Dalia was a lovely twenty-year-old woman with a beautiful face and a skin tone a little darker than my mother. At that time as a young geologist, she had received an assignment to go to western Siberia to study its natural resources. In those days, the

Russian government was interested in how energy reserves such as oil, coal, and gas might be explored in their vast rich western regions of Siberia.

I now wonder what life might have been for her. She was a dedicated Communist young woman caught up in the social and economic life of Stalin's regime. Did she survive the war? Did she ever fall in love and have a family? Did she ever think of me? It is so painfully sad for me to think that we were caught up in the turmoil and chaos of the times and never continued our relationship as sisters... I never saw Dalia again.

These memories of Dalia quickly ignited my grief for my mother and baby sister, Alya. During this time, Alya was about three years old and lived in a Soviet government nursery. I can only think that my mother probably remained in Kiev since that area was her only sense of home. I still remember her as a beautiful woman with long dark hair with striking angular facial features. I have so often wished that I had a picture of my mother, but she has remained in my mind's eye. Sadly, I saw less and less of her and little Alya...and then, not at all.

I have only compassionate feelings for my mother, for she, too, was a tragic victim of circumstances and the times we were living in. She was a broken woman in so many ways. I can only think of what my life might have been like if I had remained with her and caught in her downward spiral of depression. I hope and pray that my mother eventually found peace with her heart wrenching decision to give me to Maria. Even though there were times when I missed her terribly and longed for her presence in my life, I have forgiven her.

With passing time, I felt that I hardly knew my mother, as Maria became the mainstay of my life. Because of her determination, we managed to survive. It must have been very hard for an aging woman to take on the responsibility of caring for a young child. I could not have ever imagined then, as I trustingly began to rely more and more on Maria, that she would have a major impact on my life.

> *A father to the fatherless…is God in his holy dwelling. (Psalm 68:5, NIV)*

# Loss

I remember learning to sing a popular Soviet song that recounted the day on June 22, 1941, at exactly four o'clock in the afternoon when the German Luftwaffe (German Air Force) bombed Kiev. The song referred to the surprise attack which heavily damaged the city with a tremendous loss of lives. The song was a kind of "rally cry" against the *evil German invader* and was intended to unite the Russian people against the foe as war was declared. Everyone, including children, knew this song well. The German Army upon orders from Adolf Hitler was the aggressor, and we were told (propaganda) that Russia must defend itself. We knew that our lives would dramatically change. Many fled from the invaded Ukraine into "Mother Russia," hoping to find refuge.

As a seven-year-old child, life went on as usual that summer playing with my friends, doing chores for Maria, and surviving from day to day. However, German Luftwaffe air raid attacks were always with us and very frightening. I recall one afternoon when I was playing in a dried corn field with some of the children living near our barracks. Our play quickly was interrupted by the roar of oncoming German planes that seemed to come out of nowhere. As we looked skyward, we realized that the airplanes were flying toward Kiev again and headed in our direction. In horror, my friends and I all began to frantically run toward the barracks seeking shelter. I was wearing a red dress with matching red shoes and terrified that I might be a visible target. I did not realize that my small red dress was of no interest to a German pilot on his mission to bomb Kiev. Nevertheless, I was convinced that the pilot was coming after me. Reacting with panic, I fell to the ground and tried to hide in one of the plowed rows among the dried corn stalks. I laid there shaking and crying certain that I would be seen. I knew that I needed to internalize my fear even though I felt like screaming out loud. The planes left the sky almost as fast as they had arrived approaching Kiev. I am not sure how long I laid there trembling in terror before I composed myself to return to the barracks.

Shortly after my eighth birthday, the German army entered Kiev in September, 1941. I will *never* forget that night! To the east the city was burning, turning the night sky an orange-red; while to the west, we could hear the rumble of the German tanks. At first, we received word that the Germans burned Kiev; but later, we learned that the retreating Russian army had burned Kiev, leaving nothing of its beautiful buildings but smoldering rubble for the Germans to take. I cannot help but now wonder if the burning of Kiev was a bold Soviet Military statement to the Germans, much like when the Russians burned Moscow in 1812 as Napoleon was invading their homeland. The French army was only left with complete devastation as their conquest. So it was with the Russian army retreating from the burning Kiev; the German military just walked into the city and claimed only the smoldering ruins.

There was rampant looting among the Russian people in Kiev and panic due to the untrusting feelings they had for each other. In such desperation, some of the people were turning to crime against their neighbors. Because we were living outside of Kiev, we did not participate in the looting in the city. However, I clearly remember an abandoned warehouse not far from where we lived that stored large sacks of sugar. Maria and I walked the distance to the warehouse with great anticipation of taking as many bags of sugar as we could carry. What a treasure to have— *sweet sugar!* However, we had no other ingredients in our living space such as flour, butter, and milk to bake delicious treats. Therefore, it was not possible to have the cookies and sweet breads (paskha) that I had so eagerly anticipated eating. Isn't it interesting, that the valued thing that you think you wanted and desired so much does not always bring you the pleasure that you seek? The sugar only gave us a little "sweetness" in our lives for a brief time. This experience reminds me that destitution and loss may bring out troubling behaviors in good people. Our greed overcame our sense of right and wrong.

Living a life day to day, hour by hour, for basic survival makes you become very resourceful. I recall a time when I was wandering around the countryside, as I often did, coming upon an overgrown garden with vegetables that were over ripe and dying. I remember feeling the deep hunger ache in my stomach, as I picked the soft tomatoes to take them to Maria. How delighted she was to receive them to add to our usually thin soup! It is difficult to rationalize the difference between stealing and just being resourceful when your belly aches for food.

As the grip of the Nazi occupation tightened, the Slavic people who lived in the Ukraine felt the harsh treatment of the German officials. There were heavy restrictions placed upon them as they tried to work and provide for their families. Some of the Ukrainian people had hopes and national aspirations that the Germans might restore their country and give them a measure of independence from the Russians who felt that the Ukraine was a part of Russia. For centuries, the Ukrainians had endured Russian domination always hoping for independence!

The German occupation of Kiev was brutal, especially for the Russian Jews who lived within the city. Jewish families were beginning to feel the most *severe* treatment of the Nazi policies that restricted where they could live and work. Their plight only got worse as the German occupying government deemed them as "undesirables." When the German officials began to escalate their efforts to confine the Jews, they told them to assemble in one place and bring their clothing and valuables with them. Thinking that they were going to be "resettled" and able to live together, they did not resist. The horrors of the Nazi troops, as they systematically sought out the Russian Jewish families, revealed the tragedy of the massacre at Babi Yar, a ravine on the outskirts of Kiev. It was there that Jewish men, women, and children were stripped naked with all of their clothing, shoes, jewelry, and personal possessions to be left in piles as families were lined up to be shot. I later learned that over a two-year period, thousands of Jews were systematically murdered as they fell into the large deep ravine.

As a child, I had not witnessed the horrors that were unleashed upon the Jewish families living near Kiev. However, at night as I was lying in bed, I could hear the adults whispering and talking about the atrocities that were taking place outside of the city. Overhearing these conversations caused me to feel an anxious pit in my stomach that was very different from my hunger pains. I could not understand why the German soldiers were so angry to commit these terrible acts of violence. What had the Jews done to make the soldiers so angry? My young mind's eye could not comprehend the horrible things that were being described by some of our neighbors. I believe it was then that I began to sense that there was huge danger looming.

For a brief time during the German occupation of Kiev, our lives became somewhat easier because Maria was a "Volksdeutche," a person of German descent. Her work status and German heritage sometimes gave her privileges that our

Russian and Ukrainian neighbors did not have. I recall that one day a German officer instructed her to go through a stack of clothing that the German armies had confiscated from the Jews. I immediately sensed Maria's anxious discomfort and reluctance to approach the piles of clothing. She knew that harm might come to her if she acted disrespectful to the soldier's offer. As I watched Maria slowly approach the discarded pile, she carefully picked up a dark colored warm coat (which she greatly needed). When she turned to leave, clutching the coat tightly in her arms, I saw tears streaming down her face. This was the first and only time I ever saw Maria cry. As I now think about this painfully sad experience for Maria, I wonder if she pondered that her "new" coat came from perhaps a Jewish woman much like herself. I would like to think that Maria, thankful for the warmth of that coat, vowed to "do good in this world" in the unknown Jewish woman's memory.

Even as a child, I observed Maria's compassion and caring spirit for other people. Her social status and ability to speak the German language put Maria in the position of being someone with whom our Russian neighbors over time began feeling safe with and comfortable talking to about their problems and living conditions. When possible, Maria would go to the German authorities and advocate for their needs. Maria seemed to be everyone's "go-to person."

On occasion, Maria was repaid for her generous efforts. I remember one such neighbor who was so appreciative of Maria's positive intervention on his family's behalf with a German officer that the neighbor gave Maria his "tough old cow" which we housed in one of the storage sheds. At first, Maria was delighted to receive such a prize gift; however, she soon became bewildered as to how we would care for the cow. Fortunately, it was almost summer, and we could take the cow out of the shed to graze in a nearby field. It did not take long for Maria to realize that the cow was too old to give milk! The poor cow soon became a "gift" that Maria gave to one of the German officers for his troops. I can only imagine what a *fine "tough"* meal that old cow must have provided for the German soldiers! One *good turn* deserves another, wouldn't you say?

Anxieties and fears ran rampant among the local Russians in our barracks as news traveled that the German forces came within fifteen miles of Moscow by early December, 1941. However, the bitter cold Russian winter weather halted further German advancement, and Hitler's exhausted armies were defeated as they retreated from Moscow. It was evident that Hitler underestimated the resilience of the Russian character and military ability, as many past conquers had done before. Some of the great Russian literature may portray the people to be lyrical and poetic; but past history also shows a cruel and vicious Russian character as demonstrated by the Czars and now Premier Joseph Stalin and his mighty Red Army.

By January, 1942, we were able to acquire a second barrack room that was vacated by a family escaping into Russia. Many people tried to flee the Ukraine into Russia because of their fears of increasing invasions and the harsh treatment they thought they would experience under the German occupation of Kiev. This second room, although very small, expanded our living space. I have a memory of a large printed map of Europe hanging on a wall in that room above Artemiy's bed. As he was dying of kidney failure, our neighbors would enter the room to look at the map to determine the locations where they had heard the German armies were advancing. As I observed this happening, I realized that when people in survival mode are terrified for their own lives, they may be desensitized to those suffering around them.

Just a few months later, Artemiy died, and it was a painfully sad time for Maria and me. I do not recall when Maria prepared Artemiy's body for burial as no real arrangements were made for his funeral. I vividly remember the very bitter cold March day in 1942, when he was buried. A local farmer provided his horse and cart to transport Artemiy's corpse. I remember riding behind in the cart as Maria was sitting up front next to the farmer. We were on a bumpy and somewhat hilly road, and I remember grasping the wooden box, holding on afraid that Artemiy's casket would fall from the cart. It was difficult for me to think of the many comforting memories of Artemiy when he was alive, as I could only think of his cold body inside that roughly handmade box. I do not recall the actual location of Artemiy's final resting place as this memory is a blur for me. This was my first experience of death's reality. I felt detached and numb with cold. It was just Maria and me at Artemiy's grave site as no one else came to mourn him. My overwhelming sadness for losing Artemiy did not truly come to me for quite some time…

A positive aspect of the German occupation of Kiev was the brief restoration of the freedom of worship in the Ukraine. Where religion was previously ignored and outlawed by the Stalin regime, the German government did allow Christian worship. Religious practices were important to the Russians as they are basically people of strong faith and character. While they experienced horrific Communist rule, their faith in God endured. The Russian Orthodox Church survived, and the Germans permitted the Russian people to attend their "Tserkva," the Russian word for "church." At the age of eight, just before my August birthday, I was baptized in the Russian Orthodox Church, and Maria became my *true Godmother!* It was much later in my life when I came to realize that Maria's decision to have me baptized was a moment when she was giving me to God and dedicating me to his care.

While in Kiev during the late summer and early fall, I had the opportunity to participate in school routines. At the age of nine, I attended a make-shift school, not too far from where we lived, with eight other children ranging in ages from about eight to fourteen years old. I recall a teacher who provided us with some paper and a few books; but mostly I remember that he took us on outings in various areas outside of Kiev. Perhaps he thought that a change in scenery would be conducive to learning. He taught his lessons in Russian, and I think his primary goal was to keep us busy. His reading instruction was informal and seemed to only focus on student interest. I don't recall actually "learning to read." My true reading instruction came from Maria as she took many opportunities to read to me from a book that contained excerpts from great Russian writers such as Pushkin, Lermontoff, and Turgeniev, and others. In reality, I came to school primarily to get out of our small living space and to meet other children about my age.

I remember a family of four girls who seemed to be very hungry most every day. When I offered to share any of my bread with them, they just seemed to "fall" on the dry pieces as if they had never seen bread before. All four girls expressed their thanks to me for what little I had to give them. It is strange to say that I truly *envied* them because they were a *real family*. This was my first experience getting to know children my age and observing their close relationships as siblings. For the first time, I sensed that I lacked something in my life and wanted the bonds that these sisters seemed to have for each other. I then knew that I was a *lonely child*.

I had a very unfortunate experience with a boy about fourteen years old who was also a classmate. He lived with his family in a sod dwelling that was dug out in a nearby hillside outside of Kiev. His family had been struggling to survive for quite some time as they, too, had not been in favor with the Communist regime. Now that the German Army was occupying Kiev, his family's plight was even worse. At first, he seemed to just enjoy my friendship, and he playfully teased me as if he liked me. I was so naive and thought he was just a nice friend to be with at school—like all my other classmates. However, one day I was shattered when he inappropriately touched me and said, "I want to f— you!" I was totally bewildered and terrified! I had never encountered such aggression before. I did not realize then that he was a young maturing adolescent with his own awkward feelings and perhaps wanting to feel acceptance and love, or was it *anger*? Perhaps he was imitating some of the actions of his older sister who had a "certain" reputation in the small community. Nevertheless, this shattering experience greatly affected my young life. I felt myself "on guard" and cautious when I was around other boys and men. I guess I could say that a part of my childhood innocence was damaged.

The following day Maria noticed my unsettled demeanor as I refused to go to school. Knowing how much I was enjoying school and being with my new friends, she asked me, "What is the problem?" I struggled to tell Maria about my encounter with the boy, and I was overcome with fear and embarrassment. Maria assured me that she would not make me return to the school. What a relief that came over me as she held me close and made me feel safe. She must have understood my loss as I was very fragile and not ready to leave my childhood.

In the fall of 1942, Maria, anticipating a possible departure from Kiev to go into Poland, began to sell some of our possessions in nearby towns. I have a memory of getting on a train bound for one of the villages and carrying possessions that we thought we could exchange for food. After arriving in this small community, we stayed with a local family overnight, and the next day we traded our goods for food. As we prepared to return home, we boarded a train bound for Kiev. About forty miles outside of our home, to our dismay, the train broke down. For a moment of time, we were depending on the mercy of others around us. Fortunately, we made arrangements to stay with a local family for the night. Tired and weary, we quickly bedded down so we could rise early the next day. That morning Maria graciously thanked the family who provided us a place to rest, and she gave them a portion of our meager food supply. For me, witnessing Maria who had lost so much and left with so little, expressing her profound gratitude to the family who provided us shelter for just one night, is a powerful memory that I have internalized into the core of my being. I learned about how to express *thankfulness* to others.

In bitter cold weather, we began our walk back to the train station along a narrow roadside. As we tried to briskly walk to generate body heat, I could feel the freezing wind penetrating my clothing. We finally arrived at the train station and continued our journey home via the repaired train.

I remember that our return to the barracks felt empty and strange as Maria and I walked into our small sparse room. I missed Artemiy, and I knew Maria missed him as well. I had a strong sense that we were soon to leave this place...

> *Search me, O Lord, and know my heart; test me and know my anxious thoughts. (Psalm 139:23, NIV)*

# Poland

Very alone now, Maria decided it was time for us to escape the German occupation of Ukraine and go to Poland where her sister lived in a little town near the Carpathian Mountains. Our escape was difficult as we journeyed through various train stations along the way. The pains of hunger always seemed to our normal. Some of the German soldiers provided us with soup to eat; the very same soup that they were also eating. What kind? There is no description; all I can say is that it was edible with a combination of "several unknown things." We felt blessed to have something warm to eat.

As we traveled this difficult journey going west, we saw German troops in trains going east toward Moscow. Watching the young soldiers, as well as some much older, interested me as to where they all must have come from. I am sure they had left their homes and families feeling the stress of the war. Some of their faces looked *lost,* and some faces looked kind. Others just had blank stares of fatigue and hopelessness. They all seemed to be caught up in the drudgery and constant movement from place to place. As I reflect on these memories of these soldiers' faces and expressions, I can't help but feel that they were also victims of the war as they were only "following orders." I especially think of the young ones, perhaps the ones who lost their lives as they encountered Russian resistance; those who must have had dreams for their futures that would never come true. All these soldiers were now caught in Hitler's conquest for power. I wonder how many of those young boys and older men actually survived…

I often think of how Maria never let me feel any fear that she may have had deep inside of her being. She must have experienced feelings of terror as she anticipated the unknown. As a child, I did not truly comprehend the possible dangers of being caught up in the chaos of our survival. A child does not feel fear of the impending future. I just remember holding on tightly to her hands. Maria and I were like so many others experiencing dire hunger, bitter cold, homelessness, and enormous fatigue. There were so many times as we walked that I felt I could not take one more step. Both of us had oozing sores and sometimes bleeding blisters on our aching feet. I do not know how Maria provided for me, but somehow I had clothes to wear and shoes on my feet even though some of the shoes that I wore were terribly small for my growing feet. Baths did not come often, and we just kept moving forward. It haunts me to ponder why Maria did not ever leave me. I truly was her "extra baggage!" She could have so easily relieved herself of the responsibility and my constant basic needs by leaving me in an orphanage or in a doorway of a church for someone else to find me. Yet she must have realized that there was no future for me in the Ukraine, and her heart was open for her love to take care of me. When I think of my childlike trust in Maria, I have a memory of sitting by a window in a train car watching the snowy woods and fields of Ukraine pass by as we made our way into the mountains of Southern Poland. The rocking of the train and Maria sitting close by me is my first true recollection of a feeling of security and comfort in her care. She was truly God sent into my life.

In early December, 1942, after about two weeks of traveling by a slow moving train and walking great distances, we arrived at the home of Maria's sister. She lived with her husband and her twin adult unmarried children who were about forty years of age. Also living in their home was a younger daughter and her husband and a small four-year-old golden-haired child named Teresa. It was a full house! Maria's brother-in-law was a veterinarian who cared for local farm animals in the town and surrounding farms. Her son-in-law assisted him when he had to make animal visits.

I am sure that Maria realized that it was asking a lot of her sister to accept us into her home. We arrived weary and had not bathed in weeks. Through all the unsanitary travel, I contracted head lice. Maria's brother-in-law shaved my head with the shears that he used when he worked with his animals. This was a very traumatizing experience for me as I felt that I had lost my identity as a nine-year-old girl. For a little over a year, people mistook me for a boy.

I recall one day when I was walking on a downhill road in the rain holding a big black umbrella. As I passed a young boy from the village, he began to tease me by calling out, "You look like *kruk*!" In Polish, *Kruk* is the name of a big black bird, almost like a crow. To him, with my shaven head and the open umbrella, I must have looked like that huge black bird with expanded wings. I was completely humiliated and immediately wanted to run away.

With Maria's sister, we lived a relatively peaceful existence for about a year. I learned the Polish language and was exposed to a few books. I vividly remember Maria reading from a large book she carried with her. As her niece with her husband and brother sat at a nearby table playing cards, Maria found a small quiet corner for us to sit and read. She always seemed to have time just for me to listen to good Russian literature. I clearly remember her reading excerpts from the Russian classical author,

Lermontov, in which he wrote of a trip to the Caucasus mountains in the southeast part of Russia. His descriptive details of the scenery, the people, and their way of life seemed to be real for me in my mind's eye. Another author whose work Maria frequently read was from a lesser known writer named, Oblomov. The excerpt from his book, _Oblomovka_, also included lengthy descriptions of Russian country life. Sitting ever so close to Maria in the corner of that small room, I fondly recall the landscape pictures that I created in my head as I listened to the writers' words. The sentences that Maria read to me were elaborative and vivid to spark my imagination.

The house was not well lit, and as I think of this time, I wonder if it was difficult for Maria's aging eyesight to read to me for any length of time. She never complained, and it seemed to me that she took great pleasure in her oral reading. What a role model she was, for I began to share her passion for good literature!

When the family realized that Maria had a nine-year-old girl with her, they thought that I could take care of young Teresa and play with her. But I was very immature myself and lacked the skills to take on the responsibility of caring for a younger child. The family soon determined that they needed an older girl to help with childcare. An eighteen-year-old girl from the village came to help care for Teresa. I do not recall her name, nor do I know the arrangements for how this girl would be paid. Perhaps she was provided compensation in the form of food and living space.

One day, as we were exploring a ruined castle on a nearby hill, I remember walking down a path to the bottom of the hill where there was a local Christmas market in the village. I was totally amazed at how the market area was teaming with people everywhere selling and buying beautiful decorations such as gilded walnuts and holiday cookies in various shapes and sizes. The Christmas season and customs were not familiar to me. I did not know of Christmas and what it signified. I could not imagine what all the excitement was about.

I had much to learn, not only about the Christmas story, but also how the gift of Jesus would come to a reality in my life. I have a powerful memory of an event that occurred as I was returning home after a beautiful midnight Christmas service where I learned of the baby Jesus's birth. As we walked along the snow-laden streets with Maria and her family, we passed a multi-story apartment house. Someone in a top floor apartment was playing the violin—a beautiful melody from one of the Italian composers (perhaps Vivaldi). To my God-filled mind, it seemed to me to be the voice of an angel coming down from heaven. The melody was overwhelming to me, and I was in awe of what I heard! Falling back from the group ahead of me, I stopped to listen. I began to fill up with tears, and I realized they were not tears of sadness or self-pity. I had never cried like this before, and I felt a comforting release of "letting go." It was a soul shattering experience. In my deep inner self, a powerful emotion came over me, for this was the first time that I realized that there was more to my life than "just me alone" and my own struggle of survival to live. I feel that God was speaking to me through the strings of that violin! At that moment, I fell in love with the sound of music, and the knowledge that Jesus was with me. I did not see the instrument that night, nor did I have prior knowledge of ever hearing a violin being played before. All I knew was that it was music that I will never ever forget. Jesus, God's gift to the world, had come to me through music!

It was during that time when I began to learn more about God from Maria and her sister who was a devout Catholic. In the spring of 1943, I participated in my First Communion. I was nine years old and remember wearing a lovely white dress and veil that Maria's sister made for me. This was my first "real dress." This experience gave me a spiritual identity as a "Catholic," and I found it to be quite satisfying and an important part of my young life. As I grew in my faith over the following months, I felt a powerful devotion to God and the teachings of Jesus. Learning the Catholic rituals, I began to learn to pray.

Tensions in all of Europe were exploding, and Maria and her family realized the peril we all faced. We lived in fear of a Russian military returning into Poland and the constant activity of the partisans, the Communist guerrillas, fleeing from place to place. Maria recognized the growing intensity of the situation, and she left me with her sister to return to Kiev to take care of business. I now wonder if part of Maria's reason to return to Kiev was to make one final contact with my mother to tell her that she was intending to flee to Germany and take me with her. My thinking is that this likely happened since it was not until much later that Maria told me that while she was in Kiev for the last time, she saw my little sister, Alya, then a six-year-old still living in a twenty-four-hour state preschool. Sadly, Maria told me that Alya asked her, "Why did you save Inna? Save me too!" This was extremely difficult for Maria to tell me, and I know that she grieved over the reality of the tragic and impossible circumstances. I am sure Alya's words must have haunted her, for she had no answers for my little sister's pleading question. Maria never spoke of my mother or Alya again…

Maria, along with her sister and brother-in-law, decided that it was critically important to leave their small town and flee further into Poland from the advancing Russian army. As a nine- year-old child, I was expected to take responsibility for my few belongings. I remember that we packed our things that each of us could carry as we traveled the long distance by train to Krakow. Our trip was difficult as the train car was crowded with many refugees seeking safety in Poland. Who knows where "safety" is anymore! I just knew that I wanted to stay very close by to Maria, not wanting to let her out of my sight. When we finally arrived at the train station in Krakow, it was evident that German soldiers were everywhere according to Hitler's plan to occupy Poland and "take care" of the Jewish problem. Very weary now, we followed a street to find a place to rest. It was then that I saw the famous aged statue, "Krakow Madonna" blackened from age and the many burnings of the city. I know now that the mother of Jesus was with me.

Around Christmas of 1943, we came to live with Maria's cousin in a little isolated Polish town that did not have a railroad or even a German occupying presence. That in itself was unusual! While there, I have a vivid memory of a church service that I attended on December 31. It was a bitterly freezing day, and I recall sitting on the hard wooden church pew feeling the cold numbness of my body, hands, and feet. As I felt the intense frigid air consume my total body, I was determined to remain in prayer and self-denial to show God my total dedication to him. The long walk back alone that evening was extremely difficult as my feet and hands burned with icy pain. I felt God was in me, and it was my sacrifice of complete childlike devotion and thanksgiving for my life.

Maria's cousin owned and worked in a small pharmacy in the town, and I remember a young woman who worked for her who had a Jewish boyfriend. Once a week she would take a basket of food to him as he was living in the woods, fearful that the German SS might find him. I wonder whatever became of that young Jewish man and his Polish girlfriend... There were so many, like us, who found small ways to survive from the

German SS (*Schutz Staffel*). *Schutz* translates "protection" and *Staffel* means "division." This organization was Hitler's elite police force that rounded up many of those persons who were opposed to the Nazi Regime, especially the Jews. Hitler's terror was imposed on the Jews, then the Gypsies, and eventually the Slavs—his goal for a pure Arian race.

In February, 1944, we were hearing rumors of a large Russian army advance, and Maria, being ever vigilant, decided to go to a nearby larger town to learn more information about the worsening situation. Being of Russian descent and fleeing from Stalin's Communist regime placed us in a perilous situation. Maria knew that Hitler's rise to power was bad, but Stalin's grip on the Russian people was worse. A changing moment in my life came when I received a phone call from Maria instructing me to join her *immediately*, for the last German train was leaving in two hours, and we *had* to be on it! I did just that leaving all our meager possessions behind, wearing only the winter clothing that I had on that bitter cold day. I left with a local man whom Maria had paid to let me ride in his farm wagon to meet her at the train station.

As I look back on that fearful moment leaving everything we had, I only wish that I had thought to bring an embroidered needlework sample that Maria's young daughter created for her around 1919, just before she died. That cloth remnant was the only treasured item that Maria possessed, and I left it! Maria never spoke of it again…, but I am sure this must have pained her heart since it was the last tangible memory of her young child.

When we first boarded the train, we had good accommodations, but due to the increasingly large numbers of refugees fleeing Soviet dominance, we ended up in cattle cars with standing room only (the Jews were not the only ones to travel in this manner). Our train journey was extremely difficult with sleep deprivation, the crying of children, and the nauseating smells. The cattle car was horribly overcrowded, and many people were sick and weary of travel. I remember how terribly stressed I was whenever I felt the urge to relieve my bowels. It was terrifying to me when the train stopped, and I left the cattle car to run with others to the fields for personal elimination. I was always fearful that the train would leave without me, and I would lose Maria forever. My panic and disorientation caused tremendous stress throughout my entire body to hold my bloody bowel movements, making it difficult to run. Somehow, Maria would find me and hold me tight to calm my fear.

When we finally arrived at the eastern German border, we were herded into the close quarters of a makeshift DP (Displaced Persons) Camp for families to be processed as we were entering Germany. It seemed to me to be a big long room where each family was assigned an area. I recall the floor was made of rough unfinished boards, and each family's designated area was covered with straw. We were provided a single blanket to lay over the straw for bedding. As we were exhausted from our long travel, Maria and I were grateful to have a place to rest, meager as it was. Our pains of hunger were somewhat relieved with the thin hot soup and dried bread that was rationed to us. Thankful for this scant nourishment, we quickly devoured what was given to us. I can only remember the enormous fatigue that I felt as we both huddled together on the pile of straw to finally sleep. I felt enormous comfort to have Maria's touch and closeness.

After a few weeks, I experienced a personal feeling that I will never forget. It was the "cleansing" of my body and clothes. The Germans did not want the "dirty Slavs" to enter their homeland! They looked at Slavs as being not much better than the Jews. To expedite the bathing, families were separated and grouped by gender; men and older boys went in one direction to bathe, and women, young girls, and small children went in a different direction. There was great turmoil as family members were pulled apart from each other. As a maturing ten-year-old child, I remember taking off my clothes to be fumigated and experiencing a shower to wash my hair and body to clean myself. How awkward and vulnerable I felt as there was no privacy! There were guards watching us bathe, and I am sure that as an elderly woman, Maria must have deeply felt the degrading embarrassment, fear, and humiliation.

While at the holding camp, Maria and I met a fellow refugee who had lost contact with his wife and young son during the moment of confusion when the Germans separated families. I truly regret that I cannot recall his name. (For my reader, I will refer to this man as *Vasili*) I do, however, remember that he was desperate to reunite with his family but was unsuccessful in finding his wife and child in the mass of cramped refugees. Maria befriended Vasili and gave him hope of finding his family once we were able to board another train for Berlin since that was also his destination as well. Little did I know then that Maria's chance encounter with Vasili would have a profound impact in my future once we arrived in Berlin. I now know that God's Plan for me was in action. As a ten-year-old child, I did not know then the peril that we were facing. Maria could have so easily made the decision to leave me with her cousin in Poland. God only knows what would have become of me, for the Soviet armies were advancing, and everyone was in extreme danger. Maria was desperate to get us out of Poland and reunite with her brother's family in Berlin. She was truly my compass through this time, and I was just a trusting child. I know that the decisions and plans Maria made for us to survive were God directed.

*I have told you these things, so that in me you may have peace. In this world you will have trouble. But take heart! I have overcome the world. (John 16:33, NIV)*

# Among the Ashes of War

By the early spring of 1944, we came to live with a local farmer in Silesia, an area near the German border with half German and half Polish people (of course, the Germans were the land owners). Maria did not previously know the farmer as we were "placed" with him by the local German authorities. Our accommodations were sparse as we lived in a spare back room.

Even though we only lived there for a brief time, I was able to attend a small school in the village and once again meet other children my age. As I had left Poland in the middle of the winter, I had no light clothing as the days became warmer. Therefore, I had to go to school in clothes that some of the local people had given me—very embarrassing to a young maturing ten-year-old girl! Children are resilient beings; they don't feel deprived. However, it is when adults tell children that they are deprived, that it is when they begin to recognize and question the plight of their circumstances. Nevertheless, I felt fortunate to be able to go to school, if only for a few months. As a young student, I soon became an avid reader—*a lover of books*—which has provided me comfort for the rest of my life! School was important to me, and it was during this time that I began to study and learn the German language.

In June, 1944, Maria's goal to reach Berlin where her brother, Konrad Bonested, lived with his family was still paramount for her. Unbeknown to me at the time, Maria's health was failing. This was not surprising since Maria lived a terribly difficult life with great hardship beginning in 1919 when both her first husband and her dear nine-year-old daughter died in the same year. Losing Artemiy was a crushing loss for her as she then had to seek out our survival during dangerous times on her own. I am sure that the grueling refugee life with a young child had taken its toll on her weakening body. Yet Maria was a survivor, and she was determined that I, too, would be a survivor. As I reflect on this time, I believe that Maria likely wanted to get to Berlin to possibly seek consultation with German doctors regarding her poor health. However, the doctors were already heavily burdened with the care of displaced persons who needed immediate attention resulting from the bombings and destruction. While Maria wanted to reunite with Konrad and his family, I feel that she may have wanted to ask Konrad to take responsibility for my care in the event of her pending death. I can only imagine her heavy heart with the mental and physical stress she was experiencing.

We soon reconnected with Vasili, as he was still hoping to find his wife and son in Berlin. When we arrived in the German capital city to hopefully live with Maria's brother and family in their small apartment in Wilhelmsdorf, we were very disappointed to realize that it was impossible for us to stay. Konrad and his wife, Ella, were glad to see Maria and relieved that she was safe, but Konrad had to regretfully tell Maria that there was no room for us in their very small apartment. Ella had a young girl, Helga, born to her out of wedlock who was about seventeen years old. Ella had married Konrad in his later years, and he accepted Helga as his own child. Ella and Konrad also had two more children Klaus, age nine, and Kamilla, age six. Also living with them was Ella's older sister who was quite frail and could not care for herself. It was very evident that they could not possibly have Maria and me living with them as there were already three adults and three children for Konrad to support. It was so overcrowded there that we had to move upstairs into a vacated apartment of another family who had fled the city because of the intense bombing. Maria felt fortunate to have this place as it was close to Konrad and his family.

The former occupants of our apartment, anticipating a real famine, had dried many sacks of good German bread which at that time constituted our main diet for about six months. Hunger was always with us. Nevertheless, Maria had compassion regarding Vasili's efforts to find his family, so she offered him temporary refuge with us and shared our meager stash of food. During the day, Vasili would leave the apartment and go to the center where all refugees were to register, hoping to find his wife's name listed there. Poor Vasili, not knowing if his young family was dead or alive, was desperate to find his wife and child!

While Maria may have thought that living close to Konrad's family would be of some comfort to her, our living arrangements may have caused her additional stress. Konrad's only son was quite obviously the favored child. I recall many times when Klaus would seek out attention from his parents which usually left Kamilla in tears. It was evident that she was very insecure and needed the comfort that she sought from her mother and father. Maria seemed to sense very quickly that Kamilla was a very needy child both physically and emotionally. Maria's compassionate spirit led her to make Kamilla feel that she was loved. Therefore, Maria welcomed Kamilla to join us for our walks in the park, and on some of the outings when we searched for food. I recall a time when I sat watching Maria brush Kamilla's long brown hair, just as she had done so many times for me. I could tell that Kamilla enjoyed the special attention as Maria gently stroked her head. I think she realized that Maria was someone that she could trust and love; therefore, Kamilla began to stay with us almost on a daily basis. Thinking back on this time when I was no longer Maria's "only child," I could have helped her more in caring for Kamilla. I realize now that I was a selfish and jealous child concerned only about what I wanted and needed. As an eleven-year-old, it was hard for me to let Kamilla into my world with Maria. I was broken, and Maria was holding me together. Yet her consistent compassion and care for Kamilla, and her faithful reassurance to me that I was indeed loved, I believe, strengthened my moral conscience to learn, "This is the right thing to do!"

The days and nights were very long as we lived under constant air attacks with American airplanes bombing during the day, and the English airplanes at night. Our lives were in constant danger, and life was very precarious. Our days were spent trying to find some safety in normal routines but ever vigilant to listen for the terrifying announcements both over the radio and the outside loud speakers. Wherever we were during the day walking on the streets, waiting at the train station, traveling on the U-Bahn (underground subway), or the S-Bahn (ground railways over the city), our hearts gripped in fear when we heard the blaring sirens and announcements over loud speakers of American airplanes approaching.

*"Achtung! Achtung!"* (*Attention! Attention!*)
 *Die Luftlage Meldund.* (*Air situation announcement.*)
 *Über dem deutchum Reich gebiet feindliche Flugzeuge sind beobachtet vorden.*
 (*Enemy airplanes have been spotted over the German independent lands.*)

*Sie haben Hannover ereicht und befinden sich am Anflug auf Berlin!"*
*(They have reached the Hanover area and approaching Berlin!)*

These words meant life or death for us all as this announcement was repeated over the city, and everyone immediately understood to seek shelter. We knew the airplanes had arrived and destruction was imminent. The only safe place outside was in the underground U-Bahn, unless there was a direct hit. I clearly remember many times when people rushed to the U-Bahn which resulted with dangerous crowding and congestion. Once again, my greatest fear was losing the grip of Maria's hand and becoming separated from her in a stampeding mob.

At night, living in our small apartment, listening to the radio announcements of approaching British airplanes, we immediately ran downstairs to the basement to join other occupants of the building. There were always the sounds of young children crying, adults whimpering, and the look of fear in everyone's eyes as we heard the exploding bombs and the crashing buildings. As Maria held me close to her chest, I remember my body trembling with anticipation for the "All Clear" signal. What huge relief we all felt as we climbed the stairs back to our apartments.

Routines for survival became normal for me. Before night fall, I learned how to lay out my clothes in the order that I would put them on if I needed go down to the basement. My underwear was placed first, my dress next, socks, shoes, and my coat were last; each piece carefully in order so that I could dress myself in total darkness. I never knew when I might see daylight, and Maria taught me to be prepared.

We were ordered by the government authorities for all lights to be out at night. On very rare evenings when we had electricity for brief times, I escaped the conflict of the world by sitting in the stairway with a blanket covering a small light so that I could read German literature or my Bible. As the airplanes and bombs roared over Berlin, the earth trembled with the heavy destruction. Books and my prayers truly were my refuge and comfort during these frightful nights. Children experiencing war quickly mature beyond their years and learn to cope to survive. That was me as an eleven-year-old child!

*By day the Lord directs his love, at night his song is with me— a prayer to the God of my life. (Psalm 42:8, NIV)*

# Critical Decisions

On April 30, 1945, the Soviet army victoriously entered Berlin, and Adolf Hitler committed suicide in his bunker. The war in Europe was over! I can still remember the Russian Army celebration parade in the park near our apartment on May eighth as Berlin surrendered, and people everywhere celebrated in the streets. The Soviet Union had suffered devastating destruction and loss of lives more than any other European nation. As I sat in the window of our apartment building watching the celebrations with pompous displays of the Russian military victory over Germany, in that moment, I felt pride for my homeland.

Weeks later, Germany and its capital city, Berlin, were divided between the Allies, and Stalin's Soviet Union. Tensions were high as the conquering powers struggled to bring order to a devastated Germany. Even though all Berliners were miserably hungry, we were so glad to be free of the Nazi regime of terror.

Through all of the turmoil of the liberation of Berlin, Vasili finally located his displaced wife and their young son. The details of him reuniting with his family, I do not know, but God was working his plan for my care to be revealed within this context.

In the summer of 1945, close to the time of my twelfth birthday, Maria, my dearest Godmother, *Krosnaya* (a Russian word meaning Godmother), died at age 65. I cannot remember the details of Maria's passing except that I knew that she had been very frail and sick. She was eating less and sleeping more.

It was Konrad who told me that Maria died, and I honestly do not remember crying. It is perplexing to me that I hardly have a memory of this at all. The only memory I have is that I felt an urgency to *play*, to be outside by myself at the park near our apartment building. It is now astonishing to me to think back on this tragic and devastating time in my young life when I have very little recollection of how I dealt with Maria's death. *She was my constant, my mother, the one who saved me*! I think that I totally blocked this time from my mind as I was in denial and immersed myself in personal isolation. I recall a time when several people filled our small space in the cramped apartment, and I slipped away to be far from everyone and to just feel the fresh air outside. I do not remember what I did there, but when Konrad found me in the park, I have some recollection of him telling me that I had missed the small remembrance gathering for Maria. I believe that I was playing in the park and totally absorbed in my own world! I do not know what became of Maria's ashes, nor do I know why I reacted to her death in such a passive and isolated manner. I do not remember that I had tears—only a feeling of detachment. To make my loss more profound, Konrad felt he could not take me into his home for having his own family's needs already made it impossible for him to provide for me. I was then totally alone, *or was I?*

I now know that God was with me through it all! I am sure that Maria was a great part of his plan for me, and he remained faithful to me before I ever really knew of him. I was a "persona non grata," an unwanted person to the world—but not in the eyes of God! I probably would have been placed in a refugee orphanage had Maria not made arrangements before her death for me to live with a German lady, Anna Glinka.

It is now overwhelming to me that Maria did not know Anna Glinka prior to coming to Berlin. Their relationship only resulted because of Vasili introducing his friend, Anna to Maria. This happened when he found his wife and son in a small settlement near the train station where Anna Glinka's sister also lived. I can only imagine that Maria must have shared her plight with Anna regarding her failing heart, and her concern for what might happen to me after she was gone. It is evident that Anna felt compassion for Maria and me for her to agree to accept the responsibility of my care upon Maria's death. What an unlikely web of individuals God brought together!

Anna Glinka was a gentle woman who readily accepted me into her care after Maria's passing. I remember her telling me that she was a descendant of the great Russian composer Mikhail Ivanovich Glinka. He was regarded as the father of Russian classical opera. At that time, I knew nothing about his music, only what I remember hearing on BBC radio broadcasts from December– May in 1945. Whether she was truly related to the famous Russian musician, I will never know; but I am convinced that she was answered prayer for Maria and me!

In September, 1945, "Tante Anna" (as I fondly called her) and I lived in a single small room between two apartments in Schöneberg; the western section of Berlin occupied by the Americans. We entered our room from the outside hallway. Our living conditions were meager as the cramped room served as a bedroom, kitchen, dining area, and bathroom. A bucket served our needs, which I had to take downstairs to empty daily. In the summer, this chore was not so bad, but during the cold winter nights, it was *very unpleasant*!

Life in Berlin after the war was extremely hard and exhausting. The city was completely destroyed, and its people suffered terrible cold and hunger. Tante Anna worked in a cosmetic establishment, and there was very little money for heat and food. In the fall, we went to her sister's home in the country where we picked mushrooms and gleaned potatoes and grain, carrying what food we could from the harvested fields. There was an area around Berlin called the *Grünewald*, a German word meaning "green forest." Tante Anna and I went there to collect acorns and ground them to make coffee. The American Allies gave us large sacks of sweet potatoes cut into small dried cubes. When we received these sacks, we did not know what to do with them as sweet potatoes were not known in Germany. We decided to boil them with some fat meat resulting in an awful mess, not to mention what it tasted like! However, we survived.

On rare occasions, Tante Anna and I ventured into the eastern sector of Berlin, occupied by the Soviets. These excursions into East Berlin were a stark contrast to the life that Tante Anna and I were experiencing in the West Berlin American sector. In bleak gray East Berlin, we saw very few people out and about—people staying very much to themselves. The streets were relatively empty. In contrast to the west where we saw people seemingly enjoying a new evolving lifestyle. In West Berlin, we saw mothers casually pushing baby carriages and allowing their children to freely play in the local parks. For us and other West Berliners in the American Sector living among all the ruins in the city, there was a new liberating feeling! We saw the presence of American soldiers engaged in friendly encounters with the people, providing us with a new feeling of protection and safety. Even though we were still experiencing terrible persistent hunger, we were also experiencing feelings of "a new kind of freedom"—a feeling that I, as a child, had never had before. It seemed like another world to me to see people relaxed, sitting and talking to each other out in the open park space among the rubble of the fallen buildings and destruction from the previous bombings. I had been so consumed with my own survival and deprivation for so long, just looking for my next meal, that I had never experienced the freedom to just enjoy a beautiful day, smell the clean air, or seek out the company of others around me. Little did I realize then that the contrast between East and West Berlin would worsen as the Soviet grip on its people in East Berlin would tighten. Berliners did not realize the pending future isolation and restrictions that the Soviet Union would soon impose upon them.

In Berlin, there was an old castle-style building (Schloss Bellevue) where the Russians, the British, the French, and the Americans occupied joint offices from which they governed the city and their surrounding areas. Since Tante Anna and I lived in the American sector (Schöneberg), we were subject to the US Army authorities. It was in this building that a dramatic turning point in my life happened one day in February, 1948. I was fourteen years old when a high ranking American officer sent a car for me to come to register in his Schloss Bellevue office. What prompted this event, I will never know. Upon arrival, he told me that the Russians wanted to take me back to the Soviet Union. God only knows why—perhaps for propaganda purposes—or was it because the Soviets needed their maturing adolescent girls to replenish the population that had sadly been depleted during the war? A Soviet officer, present at the meeting and speaking only Russian, mentioned my father's name, and that is when he made a mistake. I remember bursting into tears. I had not heard my father's name voiced for such a long, long time! Stalin was still in power, and the fact that I was a daughter of an exiled writer against the current regime; I could only imagine how dreadful this situation could be for me. Upon the loss of my composure, the United States Army officer closed the meeting, and he later told me that the only safe place for me would be in West Germany or better—the United States. He explained that if I stayed in Berlin, I would never be safe and likely kidnapped off the streets by the Soviet officials as they could find me walking to my apartment from school or the park. He immediately requested a car to escort me back to Tante Anna's apartment for me to prepare to leave Berlin. Upon our arrival and hearing this news, Tante Anna helped me gather my few belongings and tried to reassure me that I would be taken care of by the Americans. I could hardly comprehend what was happening to me as it was all occurring so fast! The American officer was so serious, and his urgency for me to leave was terrifying to hear. I had no idea where they were taking me! My body was numb with fear.

As I think back on these horrific memories, I realize now what a hero this American officer was to me. I truly believe God placed him in my life to make some critical decisions for my safety when no one else around me could. Oh, how I wish I knew what became of him! I don't even know his name! The deliberate and proactive measures he took to warn me of the Soviet officer's intent, and the danger I was in at that time are overwhelming to me now. I was so young and so vulnerable! He truly saved my life by making arrangements for me to go to a transitory DP Camp Marienfelde, in Berlin close to the Tempelhof Airfield.

Ever so sadly, I had to leave my beloved Tante Anna. How could it be that morning when she greeted me as I awoke from my bed, that by the early evening I would be torn from her arms? We tearfully parted as I abruptly left West Berlin from the Tempelhof Airfield on a C-47 cargo plane that had arrived after delivering Army supplies. It was haunting to me to not know whatever became of Tante Anna. As a fourteen-year-old girl, but still a child, I was so absorbed and consumed in my own personal crisis that I failed to continue communications with her. Oh, how I terribly regret that we lost each other in the turmoil of my departure. Tante Anna came into my life when I needed someone to rescue me, and I owe her so much for caring for me after Maria died. I grieved for losing Tante Anna, and when I did experience that grief, I finally allowed myself to grieve for the loss of Maria as well. I will never understand how these two women came into my life and were so vital to my survival. I will always believe that they were truly my "earth angels."

*Why are you downcast, O my soul?*
*Why so disturbed within me?*
*Put your hope in God, for I will yet praise him,*
*my Savior and my God. (Psalm 42:5, NIV)*

# New Beginnings

As I left Berlin, and for the first time in my life, feeling a huge airplane lifting me into the air, I felt my world had truly fallen apart. I was completely overwhelmed as I experienced the turbulence inside of the C-47 airplane. I sobbed deeply to my core knowing that I might not ever return. I had never before felt the burning of tears in my eyes as I did then. The loud roaring of the plane's engines and propellers, as well as the bumping feeling in the cabin, created a very unsettled sensation in my stomach. When we finally arrived at the airfield in Frankfurt/Main in West Germany, the refugees, officially called Marienfelde Displaced Persons (DPs), began to disembark from the plane. What a relief it was to feel the solid ground below my feet. I recall a US Army soldier guiding me to a jeep that was bound for the DP Camp. I remember riding in the jeep with two Jewish young people chattering in Yiddish, confident in the knowledge that they were not understood. However, Yiddish being similar to German, I understood them quite well! I soon realized that the Jewish children never stayed in camp for any length of time since they soon found homes in their new developing nation of Israel and America.

On June 20, 1945, I was transferred from DP Camp Marienfelde to the DP Camp Aglastarhausen (near Heidelberg), which was operated by the United Nations. The small camp was adequate, as the Americans provided food and shelter. There were only about two dozens of us ranging in ages from two to seventeen years old. Thus, we were a very close group, despite our diverse backgrounds and ages. However, there were more Russians and Jewish teenagers among the group.

We participated in dances and other group entertainment. I remember one Lithuanian girl who was a very good dancer and very friendly to me. I was so impressed with her and her agile movements. This was my first opportunity to experience dancing, and my feet just seemed to not move in the direction that I wanted them to go. I felt so awkward, and she seemed so graceful! I was amazed to hear that she later left for America to become a Catholic nun. I often wondered how someone as lively and full of energy as she was could live a strict cloistered lifestyle. I do not recall her name, but my memory of her is that she seemed to be a young woman full of faith and dedication—a gentle spirit to me.

During the fall of 1948, I was transferred from Aglastarhausen to Bad Aibling, another DP Camp, south of Munich near the Bavarian Alps. I had just turned fifteen years of age in August, and I still remember seeing those huge mountains for the first time in my life! In the beginning, as I gazed in the distance, I thought them to be a large bank of clouds on the horizon. But the next morning, they were still there; I only then realized that they were indeed *mountains—very high mountains!*

I stayed in Bad Aibling, a former German S.S. (Schutz Staffel) Camp, for a year waiting for the opportunity to go to the United States. We were separated by nationalities and religions. This was an effort to preserve the refugee orphans' heritages. Thus, I lived with Ukrainians who were primarily Russian Orthodox. During this time, I began to study the English language and had the opportunity to enjoy time with a Baptist Church missionary fellowship group of other young people about my age. This group greatly influenced my spiritual awareness of Jesus as my Savior, and I soon began to identify myself as a devout Baptist. This was the first time I felt a true *personal relationship* with God. I had a strong sense that God was with me, and he not only had a plan for me, but he was also leading me to witness my faith to others.

My friends and I were so hopeful of a better life in the United States. It was here that I met Michael Kuzma, a boy that I imagined to be the love of my life! We were good friends and enjoyed our time together sharing stories and "Spanish Ronda"—a promenade dance of a line of girls and a line of boys, meeting together and nodding and smiling—such adolescent fun! I think this was the first time in my life that I "blushed" and enjoyed the company of the opposite sex! All I had ever known before was being in a *survival mode*, and now I was experiencing the pleasure of "getting to know boys," laughing, sharing stories with others my age, and *dancing*! I also met a dear girl, Jadwiga Botcharenok, a Ukrainian-Polish girl who truly was my first *real friend*. I had never experienced friendship before! What a liberating experience it was to share these moments and live life with others my age!

In early March, 1949, I had a very painful sore throat that was getting worse and worse; so painful that I was sent to a hospital in Munich where I stayed for two months. After high fevers and weight loss due to my recurring throat infections, the doctors determined my tonsils needed to be removed. During my absence while in the hospital, Michael was sent to America, and I believed that I had lost him forever. I felt extremely depressed that I had not only lost touch with Michael, but also that I would likely never see him again! I also feared that I may have lost some of the dear friends that I had in the Bad Aibling camp. This was devastating to me as I felt so very lost and alone in my hospital room. I had never known *friendship* in my life before my DP camp experience, and I feared that I was returning to a life of isolation having lost all my friends. It was not until I was finally discharged from the hospital in early June that I returned to the Bad Aibling camp. It seemed so strange to realize that all my friends were gone to America or Australia, and I once again felt terribly alone. However, one day as I was walking in a new section of the camp, I saw my old friend, Jadwiga, from a distance. I could not believe my eyes as I was shouting her name and running toward her waving my arms to get her attention. She was as surprised to see me, as I was to see her. After tearful hugs, I realized that I was not alone, and that finding a *lost* friend was like finding a treasure. During my recovery and absence from the camp, there were many new refugee arrivals, and I soon realized that I could make new friends easily.

The Soviet government was very aggressive in the pursuit of returning their displaced Russian and Ukrainian refugees back to their homelands. Since 1946, the "Iron Curtain" was becoming a reality across the middle of Europe with the eastern counties under Soviet domination. Little did I realize the peril I was in at that time! My life was forever changed by a miracle encounter with a Russian Orthodox priest whom I met in the camp. One day, he sought me out to explain to me that because I did not have a sponsor or family members in the United States, my chances to go to America were very unlikely. He told me that as a maturing young woman of childbearing age, I would surely be returned to the communist Soviet Union. I was devastated! How could God have brought me this far and then have me return to a hostile homeland? I could only pray...

Days later, God's plan was revealed to me when the priest returned telling me that since I was baptized as a young child in the Russian Orthodox Church and that he knew my father, he would provide me with the appropriate documentation advocating for me to go to the United States of America! I am not sure how this priest could have possibly known my father other than he knew of his writings and Leninist activities that threatened the Stalin regime years ago. Nevertheless, he made the paperwork happen!

In November, 1949, when I was sixteen, my world completely changed for it was then my time to go to the United States of America! I still remember that wonderful night with the moon overhead when I flew in an airplane over the Atlantic Ocean anticipating a better life in my new country, *America!* I could only imagine that the streets were paved with gold! Childhood memories flooded my mind: my mother pulling my sled through the knee-deep snow in Kiev; picking cherries for a farmer in Silesia (half of them going into my mouth, for I loved cherries); watching a group of joyous young Jewish men at the Tempelhoff Airport in Berlin going to Israel! I wonder what became of them in that war-torn country. Just watching the joy on their faces as they looked forward to a new life; their total exuberating expressions and happiness inspired me to have my own hopes for a brighter future in the United States. Not all of my memories were bad, for a child's mind does not dwell on such things, a child just moves forward. And that is just where I was, moving forward with new dreams for my life. Would I have a family some day? Would I find love and acceptance? Would I have a purpose in my life? These were all questions… I now realize were my silent prayers. God was with me and gave me hope for the future. I truly felt unafraid and open to whatever may happen. I finally felt *free to dream!*

> *Though I walk in the midst of trouble, you preserve my life; you stretch out your hand against the anger of my foes, with your right hand you save me. (Psalm 138:7, NIV)*

# Another World

My fellow refugee orphans and I arrived in New York City in November, 1949. For about six weeks, we lived in the Bronx in an old abandoned Jewish synagogue overlooking a polluted river. There was a dried riverbed that was filled with old beat-up cars, refrigerators, and other thrown away refuses. What a shock this was to see that the "golden America" that I had dreamed of was so full of debris. Looking at the dirty water, I wondered why Americans were dumping waste and trash into such a precious resource. The wonders of American life amazed and saddened me at the same time. I was astonished at the carelessness with which Americans thoughtlessly consumed so many resources which in Europe were so scarce such as food, electricity, transportation, and a city alive with light—all blessings of a rich life! I was totally unprepared for witnessing the abundance and the waste. This reality troubled me greatly.

In Europe, I was so used to having a very meager selection of food or none at all! During the war, I ate anything that I could—now, I was overwhelmed with the selection of food—olives, pickles, oranges, and apples that were provided for us by the United Nations. Shortly after we first arrived, I remember a Jewish friend exclaiming, "*Oh, olives!*" It was the first time I had ever seen an "olive," and I was amazed to eat such a thing! Tasting new foods became an adventure for me. Praying for God's blessing of food before a meal was powerful for me.

While waiting for American families to hopefully adopt us and provide us *real* homes, my newly found refugee friends and I took classes to learn American ways of life and improve our English skills. We were eager to venture out into the big city to see the sights, watch the people, and experience going to parks and museums. It soon became evident to me that New York City was a place of two different worlds—one for the rich and one for the abandoned and neglected. As I walked along the bustling city sidewalks, I observed people seemingly preoccupied with where they were going and impatient to reach their destinations. I saw destitute individuals sleeping in doorways or on sidewalk grates for warmth. *Poverty was in America!* I had not anticipated the poor begging out in sight. I saw food lines much as I had seen in Berlin. I was unprepared for seeing the real America that I had fantasized to be so different. There were so many cars and so many crowds of people! I was truly feeling a culture shock, and staying close to my refugee friends relieved much of my anxiety.

As this was December, there was much to see in the big city area of New York. What overwhelmed me the most were all the lights *everywhere*. As I remembered the city streets of Berlin at night, there was total darkness. Even during the day, very few lights were on. In sharp contrast, grand New York City displayed elaborate holiday decorations. I was amazed to see so many bright colored lights—*all colors!*

When my friends and I ventured into some of the large department stores, we were amazed and a little saddened by all the enormous displays of clothes, jewelry, shoes, other personal items such as women's make-up and beautiful hats. The abundance was beyond what we would ever have imagined! All of this was so very different from the "big" shopping center of

Berlin, Kurfustendam, which was much smaller with only items of basic needs and some new fashions.

As new arrival refugees under the auspices of the United Nations Relief and Rehabilitation Administration (UNRRA), we were given opportunities to meet various people who were interested in making contributions for our care. I recall being invited to several Christmas parties sponsored by various businesses and organizations. These parties were held in tall high-rise offices and apartments where there were lavish foods and entertainment. While there were many people who I am sure meant their sincere concern for us as orphans, I soon began to feel like we were objects of pity. Therefore, it was not long until I refused such invitations. I did not want people to feel sorry for me as I was proud of my European heritage and background. I knew, despite the terrible war, that I had *survived* and had much to offer in my life. Rather than people giving me elaborate parties with over abundant foods and gifts (such as a cashmere sweater that I once received), I truly wanted them to listen to me and learn more about me as a person. I so much wanted to connect with Americans and establish friendships to know more about their lives. Even with my broken English, I wanted to be seen not as a poor refugee, but as a valued individual with hopes and dreams for citizenship and my future in this blessed land. I soon realized that making personal connections in my new surroundings was more difficult than I had anticipated.

While I was with many of my friends from the DP camp in Bad Aibling, I missed seeing Michael and my dear friend, Jadwiga. However, I soon learned that Jadwiga had been adopted by a Polish family living in the Cleveland, Ohio, area. I felt happy for her as she was of Polish descent herself and to find parents of similar background seemed to me to be a perfect match. While we did lose communication with each other, I remember her fondly as she was my *first real friend.*

Michael came to the United States while I was in the hospital in Munich, Germany, and for a time, we were unable to communicate with each other as he had joined the US Air Force. To my surprise, for my first Christmas, 1949, in the United States, Michael sent money to some of our refugee friends who lived in Philadelphia for them to come to New York City to take me out to see a *movie in a theatre!* What a generous and thoughtful thing for him to do for me and our friends. Somehow I knew that I would see Michael again…

This was a time when my new country, the United States of America, and the Soviet Union had emerged as the new superpowers of the world. The *Cold War* now existed with the threat of nuclear war. I did not realize at this time in my life what this all meant, but the tensions between the US and the Soviet Union would have a great impact for my future plans.

*The Lord will fulfill his purpose for me; Your love, O Lord, endures forever— do not abandon the works of your hands. (Psalm 138:8, NIV)*

# A New Life with New Challenges

I was adopted in February, 1950, by Dr. and Mrs. Leon Gardner who at that time lived in Washington, DC. I will never forget the anxious anticipation I felt boarding a train leaving Grand Central Station in New York City bound for Washington. My "new mother," whom I had never met, was to meet me at the Union Station. I knew to look for a lady dressed in a Red Cross uniform as she would be arriving at the station after she left her place of work. It was an awkward greeting when I met Margaret Gardner, as she was a much older woman than I had expected. I noticed that she did not embrace me as her new daughter but began to "chatter" about how happy she was to see me. We both were not sure about "a hug." It was certainly not the familiar European greeting with a kiss on both cheeks. I quickly learned that this form of greeting was *not* in character for my new mother. She seemed to me to be a very "stiff" woman and serious in her demeanor with "prim and proper" mannerisms.

I only had a single bag with me and a very worn coat which I had received as a "gift" in New York City. As we walked to her Red Cross car, I felt totally overwhelmed. I clearly recall the drive home, as she drove down Georgia Avenue and passed a large building. As she slowed the car down for me to look at the building, she announced, *"This is Nonna's school!"* I had the sense that she thought I knew who "Nonna" was, and that I should be impressed that "Nonna" had her own school! This comment completely confused me and caused me to feel on edge and more nervous.

We soon arrived at Van Buren Street off of Sixteenth Street, not far from the Walter Reed Hospital. As we approached "my new home," I quickly saw that the surrounding homes seemed enormously large, and I thought that people of wealth must live in them. I was again feeling unsettled anticipation as she drove into the driveway of an imposing brick home with white trim and beautiful trees and a manicured yard. As we entered the arched front door of this lovely home, I saw an enormous amount of furnishings—beautiful chairs and sofas with plush materials and soft cushions and pillows. The wooden floors were clean and buffed to a shine. There was a large dining room table and chairs that would seat many guests. As I looked around the living room, I saw a large grand piano. I immediately had a quick flashback of Artemiy in our cramped small room in Kiev and how he so wished that I could learn to play such a fine instrument. Oh, if he could see me now!

The entire house was filled with beautiful objects on tables and mantles. I had never seen such a home! Was I truly going to *live* here? Numerous pictures and paintings were displayed on the many walls in the house. It was evident that my new mother was especially fond of old English hunting scenes of gentlemen in top hats and finely cut hunting coats with ladies riding side saddle. These pictures of the English hunt were all over the house! I found them to be quite interesting but very odd. Having no knowledge of English history, I did not understand the aristocratic old English sport of hunting with dogs and horses. It was strange to me to see pictures of people dressed in such elaborate clothing going out just to hunt a fox! As I became more settled in my new home, I frequently walked around the house studying and admiring these curious paintings. As time went on, I began to learn more from my mother about English customs and history, and I soon gained an appreciation for the artists' work and talent.

Upon my arrival, the first day, Margaret guided me through the hallways to the room where I would sleep. There were two beds and my "new mother" explained to me that I would share this room with *"Nonna,"* I remembered that name from our drive from the train station, but I had no idea who this *"Nonna"* was! I would later learn that afternoon when Nonna came home from school that she would be my new *sister*.

As I look back on this first experience to my new home, I am amazed that Margaret seemed to feel that I was "connecting the dots" or understanding what was happening. She was wrong to think that immersing me into a new and strange environment would be so easy. Far from the truth! I felt *totally* out of place and completely disorientated.

Margaret quickly began to show me a closet and a chest of drawers for me to store my belongings. I thought it odd that she assumed that I needed so much room for my few possessions! However, at this time, my need was greater than just putting clothing in drawers; I needed to relieve myself! How awkward I felt not knowing where to find a toilet! I truly cannot remember the details of this experience other than somehow I found my way to a bathroom—what an experience that was! Not only did I find a toilet, I also found a large shiny white tub, a separate shower, a sink with a lovely mirror, and numerous plush soft towels hanging around the bathroom area. This truly was unheard of for me. I was shocked as I could hardly believe what I was seeing—a whole room about the size of half of the room where Maria and I lived in Ukraine.

My new adopted father, Leon Gardner, was born in China to American missionaries from New England. He was a well-educated man and a physician in the US Army. I have such a memory of our first meeting on the day I arrived. When he came home from work, he walked down the hallway and into the room where I was putting my things away in the chest of drawers. He greeted me with a friendly *"Hi!"* At that time, I did not know who he was and how to respond to him; therefore, I quickly turned away and remained silent. It was later when Margaret came to me and asked me why I did not respond when my "new father" greeted me. I told her that I did not know who he was, and I did not understand what he was saying to me. I did not know that "Hi" meant "Hello". Thus, began my confusing misunderstandings of the complicated English language!

Almost immediately on my first day in my new home, I met *another* member of the Gardner family—the dog "George!" What a beautiful and well-groomed Cocker Spaniel he was! His shiny black-and-white coat was soft and brushed daily, and needless to say, he was spoiled beyond belief! He truly reined the household! George was not a new puppy as he had been with the Gardner family for many years. He had his own special routines of coming and going in the house and his own space for enjoying his leisurely naps. One thing for sure was that he was *not* underfed! Because of his age, he was not very playful so you could say that he was "fat!" George and I immediately became friends, and he was the first animal that I had ever cared for and loved. He truly gave me his unconditional love. I found comfort in having George close by me and stroking his soft shiny coat and feeling the warmth of his body beside me. I soon took on the responsibility of walking George every day after school on Van Buren Street with its gently downhill slope and large shady trees.

I immediately began to call Margaret and Leon, "mother and father," at their insistence. I so much wanted their loving attention and approval. Prior to my adoption, the Gardner family had already adopted two other girls, Jeannie and Nonna. The thought of having two sisters was exciting to me as I anxiously awaited meeting them.

Later in the day, I had my first encounter with Nonna, my "new sister," who was two years older than me. She came through the front door after walking home from Calvin Coolidge High School; the building on the hill off of Georgia Avenue that Margaret had pointed out to me earlier as we were riding home from the train station. Nonna was aware of my adoption, so I was no surprise to her when she arrived. Upon meeting Nonna, I was elated to think that I had a *real sister*. Nonna was polite but not seemingly overjoyed to see me. It did not help for her to observe me unpacking my few belongings and putting them in *her* chest of drawers. It was understandable that sharing her space with me was not a pleasant thought for her. I wanted so much to bond with her as a real sister and to share our common backgrounds. I had instant flashbacks of the four little sisters playing in the school yard in Kiev and how I was longing for a real family. To me, Nonna was my hope for having a loving sister-bond. However, I soon learned that her manner was far from welcoming. It was very disappointing to me to realize that she felt anger toward me from the very beginning. I felt that Nonna could not get pass her lingering resentment that I was sharing *her* bedroom and was intruding into *her* place in the family. I recall having flashback memories of when I was eleven years old with very similar feelings as Nonna. I remember how I felt when Maria invited little Kamilla into *my* space in Berlin. I found it very difficult to accept the caring attention that Kamilla was receiving from Maria.

Living in the same space was difficult for both of us. I have a memory of me sitting on a hassock in our room, playfully trying to get Nonna's attention as she walked pass me. I teasingly tried to "snag her skirt" with my leg, and she immediately turned on me and shouted, "I am going to smash you in the *morda!*"—a degrading Russian word meaning the *snout of an animal.* My disappointment was deeply felt as I thought, "So this is my loving sister?" My humiliation was not only felt by me alone. In the early days after my arrival, I discovered that Jeannie, our *older sister* who was soon to be married, also felt the brunt of Nonna's abusive words.

To my dismay, Nonna and I never bonded to share our lives with each other as close sisters. As I look back on those difficult years living with Nonna, I think about where she was in her life at the time. I do not blame Nonna for her actions toward me, for she, too, had suffered in her earlier life. She had a story as well. She, like me, lost her mother at a very early age during the war. The woman who became her stepmother was very cruel and likely mistreated her. Nonna may have felt that she was an unwanted child under the "foster" care of her stepmother. Nonna's father was an officer of the Soviet Red Army and was possibly killed during the war. She, too, must have felt abandoned. As I now ponder my relationship with Nonna, I realize that she was also a product of her Russian background, much like me. She had very little prior cultural experiences and greatly lacked appropriate American social behavior. I think that her verbal outbursts at me reflected her early life. What a shame that we were both so hurt from our past experiences that we could not become closer. I think we both were still in "survival mode." There was an emotional wall that neither one of us could break through to find a friendship, much less *sisterhood.* Now, many years later, I can only wish that I could have somehow reassured Nonna that I was only *sharing her space, not taking her place.*

After a very short time in my new home, Leon began to question my true age. He decided to go through the court system to change the year of my birth from 1933 to 1935. As a physician, he determined that my physical development did not seem to justify the earlier date. Could he not have realized that my physical underdevelopment was caused by my early years of *malnutrition*? The war years were hard on my young body. I now believe my father wanted to change the date of my birth due to his desire for me to be at the age level of my ninth grade classmates. Because he was now my parent, "in charge of my care," I accepted his decisions trusting that he knew what was best for me. However, his decision affected me for the rest of my life and created consequences such as when I was sixty-five and ready to apply for Social Security, my US documents indicated that I was just sixty-three!

Margaret was head of the Red Cross at St. Elizabeth Hospital; a mental facility for patients who had experienced critical trauma or "shell shock" during the war. Her position in the Red Cross put her in frequent contact with First Ladies, Eleanor Roosevelt and Bess Truman. Margaret knew Eleanor Roosevelt during the war years when the first lady was promoting the work of the American Red Cross. She greatly admired her and emulated Mrs. Roosevelt's passion for helping the less fortunate.

While the Gardners focused on providing me with excellent education and cultural opportunities for a better life, I desperately wanted a mother's loving touch and affection. I soon realized that my new mother was a very busy professional lady who had little time for me as I was adjusting to life "on my own." I vividly remember one evening when I saw my mother lounging on her bed reading a book. As I crept into her room, I immediately went to "cuddle" close beside her. I wanted to feel the closeness to her as I had felt with Maria when I was a young child. Her body language was complete rejection. It was evident that she wanted to be alone in the solitude of her reading and relaxation after a full day of work. I soon came to know my place in the family.

My relationship with Leon should have been closer. I so much wanted to connect with him as a father, but my past experience as a young child in Ukraine with the boy at my school shadowed my confidence in men. The Gardners wanted their girls to "forget" their prior lives and any bad experiences they may have had in Europe. They wanted us to become immersed in the American culture and put our prior life experiences behind us. Nonna seemed to be able to do that, but I could not. I was still struggling to *survive!* Nonna controlled our father, and I recognized that I could not enter into their bonded circle. Nonna also had Leon's favor because of their common interest in the medical field, especially human physiology. She and my father engaged in long discussions as he tutored her in a field of science that he knew a lot about and had a great interest in sharing. Nonna in later years became an Occupational Therapist, which gave the Gardners great pride. Nonna seemed to "fit in" with the Gardners' lifestyle because she appeared to be able to let go of her past—while I was still clinging to my past. It was a very difficult and challenging transition for me.

Learning to live within a family unit, taking on the roles of a child with two parents, and being a sister to two siblings presented challenges for me that I had not expected. For example, I was not in the habit of daily hygiene routines in my life because bathing was a *"whenever I can"* experience in Europe. I now was expected to follow Nonna's example of taking a nightly bath in a *real* bathtub! I remember how amazed I was to run hot water into a large white shiny tub, just for *one person* to get into to *wash one single body*! While this should have been a relaxing comfort for me, I actually felt traumatized to be in a tub full of water—precious clear water. It seemed such a waste!

I soon learned that American girls shaved their legs. Upon arrival, I had very hairy legs, for shaving legs was not a customary thing for young girls and ladies in Europe. I had no idea as to how to acquire a razor and even begin to take on the task of shaving my legs! Nonna was very critical of my appearance, and I knew that I had to change. I recall watching Nonna use a razor and carefully shave her legs. Oh, how I longed to obtain a razor of my own, but I did not know how! I soon acquired the courage to ask my mother for a razor. She quickly found a new razor for me to use and showed me how to carefully insert the razor blade. It almost seemed like a weapon to me, but as I glided the razor over my soapy lathered legs, I soon felt accomplishment to feel my smooth skin. To this day, I remember the emotional turmoil that I felt as I learned to take care of my personal care and hygiene.

Another problem for me was learning how to put on nylon stockings. At that time, ladies and young girls wore "nylons" with the seams going up the back of the legs. I knew that it was imperative that I get the seams straight! This required an inspection from Nonna, which frequently did not go well. American women had sacrificed wearing nylons to support the war effort, and now nylons were more plentiful in the early 1950s. I remembered that in Europe, women would do "anything" to ask the Allied soldiers to give them nylon hosiery; such a delicate fabric and wearing them was considered to be a high fashion statement. I felt such success as I admired my "seams" in the full length mirror!

I knew that I had *plenty*, as I was surrounded by so many material objects and things everywhere in the house, but having "so much" presented its own problems. I often felt a high sense of anxiety being around so much *abundance*. This created another huge challenge for me as I was resisting my strong impulse to hoard food. My new mother was originally from California, and her mother would send our family beautiful baskets of lovely fruit and nuts. I remember thinking how perfect the California fruits looked—so shiny, perfectly formed, and smooth! When my mother kept these fruit baskets in the cool basement, I would venture down the stairs to take some of the fruit and nuts and hide them under by pillow. I recall one day when my mother received a beautiful box of chocolates. I had never seen such a lovely display of chocolate candy! I recall that I felt enormously compelled to take a few chocolates and instinctively hide them under my bed sheets. How shamed and totally embarrassed I felt when my mother discovered that the melted chocolates had stained and ruined her beautiful satin quilts. I can still see those soiled linens in my mind today!

As a refugee, I basically had no responsibilities in my life but to survive in war-torn Europe. Survival during those early years was enormously difficult—a matter of life and death. Now, my survival *seemed* almost as great but *very different!* I was in a home environment where I was given daily family responsibilities to help around the house. Some of my daily duties were to make up my bed, gather clothes to be washed and taken to the laundry room, and to help wash the dishes after a meal. Nonna and I would take turns washing and drying the dinnerware. I remember how overwhelmed I felt seeing the large kitchen cabinets full of beautiful china with various sizes of dinnerware such as glasses, plates, and bowls. It was hard to comprehend—*Why so much?* I have a memory of Nonna taking a glass from the cabinet and pouring herself some fresh orange juice. After she had taken a sip from the glass and placed it on the table, I immediately without thinking, took her glass and drank some of the remaining juice as well. Nonna was enraged at me wanting to share her glass of juice! I did not understand why she was so upset about me drinking from her glass. I had spent my childhood having to share one glass or cup with others, and to me, this behavior seemed normal. In Europe, I was unaware of "germs," and I certainly had not learned customary social table manners. Oh, how painful it was to adjust to my new family life style! *Will I survive all of this?*

My new parents wanted to provide as many artistic and cultural opportunities for me as possible. Thus, I began my piano lessons. My teacher lived close by on Georgia Avenue, and I could walk to her house. She had a spacious home with a baby grand piano, much like the one the Gardners' had in their living room. I am afraid that my piano teacher realized very early on that I had no talent! I must have been a huge challenge for her. However, she was very patient with me and tried to help me feel at ease at the keyboard. I was still learning the English language that was built on the Latin alphabet and was intrigued that the music staff and the arrangement of the piano keys also reflected the English alphabet with the letters A, B, C, D, E, F, and G. I practiced my music daily and labored to repeat the musical phrases with my fingers in the correct positions. Even though my progress was very slow, I soon found my efforts to play a tune to be very satisfying. Practicing my music lessons offered me time to myself, and I felt the resonating tones of the piano to be so lovely and comforting.

Living in the magnificent capital city of my new country, Washington, DC, with all its grand monuments, statues, and huge marble buildings also created huge problems for me. I recall a time when Nonna and her boyfriend, who was very playful and friendly (Leon teasingly called him Bojangles!), invited me to join them for a ride in his new car. "Bojangles" was eager to drive us all around the DC area to proudly show me the beautiful city. How frustrating it was to see the historical sights and not know the history that they symbolized. I did not know who Thomas Jefferson and Abraham Lincoln were. However, it was evident to me that they must have been very important men to have such magnificent structures built in their honor. I felt so overwhelmed to be in this impressive place and not know anything about it. I marveled at how clean the city appeared to me for I had just left the blackened ruins and rubble of Berlin. The Washington government buildings were incredibly white and shining, especially in the sunlight, and they seemed to glow at night with perfectly placed lighting. I just felt extremely grateful to be in my new beautiful country!

My parents were generous in offering me many educational opportunities, and I am forever thankful to them. One such opportunity happened at the time of my first Christmas with the Gardner family in 1950 when Michael Kuzma, the boy I met in the Bad Aibling DP Camp, came to Washington, DC, to visit me for the holidays and to meet the Gardner family. During his visit, my mother received tickets from Bess Truman to attend a Brahms Concert in Constitution Hall and sit near the US Presidential box. This frequently happened when the President and the First Lady had other commitments and could not use their tickets. This gesture from Mrs. Truman was in accordance with continuing her support of Eleanor Roosevelt's passion for the work of the Red Cross. What an unthinkable experience it was for both Michael and me to be sitting in the seats of US Presidents! We were just two poor refugees who spent the previous Christmas in a DP Camp not knowing if we would *ever* go to the United States of America! And here we were in all the grandeur of a magnificent concert hall!

During Michael's holiday visit, we enjoyed seeing more of the Washington sites, meeting a few of my new Russian friends, and reminiscing over the times we experienced with our mutual refugee friends in Germany. It was good to know that Michael was happy with his new military life in the US Air Force. How proud he was to wear his uniform! When he returned to his military assignment, I soon realized that long distance communication with Michael was sporadic and not easy. I found it difficult to read his letters because he wrote them primarily in the Ukrainian language with some English slipped into his correspondence. He, too, was struggling with learning his new language. While the Russian and Ukrainian languages are similar, there are minor differences that caused me frequent confusion and frustration. I soon acquired a big stack of letters from him which I intended to read at some future time, but sadly, they remained in my chest of drawers. We both were experiencing many complicated challenges and adjustments to our new American lives.

As time passed and my routines became more and more familiar to me, I began to learn to cope and focus on my own day-to-day living.

> *Be strong and courageous. Do not be afraid…*
> *for the Lord your God goes with you; he will*
> *never leave you nor forsake you. (Deuteronomy*
> *31:6)*

# Will I Ever Fit In?

Soon after arriving to the Gardner home at the age of sixteen, but "on paper, age fourteen," I was placed in the ninth grade at Paul Junior High School not far from the Walter Reed Hospital. Nonna was completing her junior year at Calvin Coolidge High School. Unfortunately, she did everything she could to make my transition to a structured school setting difficult. She withheld helpful information that created times that proved to be embarrassing and awkward for me. I found it hard to ask her questions about general school routines and student movements in the hallways. When I probed her to tell me about how she carried her books from class to class, she quickly responded, "You'll find out!" I remember one of my first days shortly after I arrived at my new school; I was eating lunch in the cafeteria with others in my class. At the end of the lunch period, two American girls showed me how to remove my lunch tray. I was horrified to see the students dumping their leftover food into the trash cans—mounds of good food that they had hardly eaten—thrown away! Seeing this caused me to burst into tears, and I completely lost my composure. I could only remember scavenging for whatever I could eat in the Gruennewald forest around Berlin to comprehend and accept the waste that I was seeing before me! For me, food is so precious!

There were so many times that I felt as if I was drowning in my new school environment. *I survived World War II in Europe;* how could I not find my way on so many levels in a school setting with people I did not understand! I experienced tremendous learning gaps because I lacked a significant education background and complete knowledge of the English language. I was completely unaware of teenage social life in America. Had it not been for three girls who befriended me—American students Elizabeth Weber and Jane Williams and a Slovenian girl Bozhana Trost—taking me under their care to teach me about my new school and social environment, I am not sure that I would have survived the whole school experience.

It was Bozhana who endeared herself to me as we had much in common. How ironic it is that the Slovenian meaning of her name is "one who is desired!" Bozhana and I, both of Slavic descent, felt a special connection that bonded us as dearest friends. In the early 1930s, Bozhana's father brought his young wife to the United States for him to work in New York City at the Royal Yugoslav Consolate. Bozahana was born shortly thereafter. When World War II began, he was then transferred to Washington, DC, to work in the Yugoslav Embassy as the Assistant Commissioner for shipping, immigration, and emigration. Bozhana's mother became like a second mother to me. Because of her Slavic heritage, she helped me to better understand the American culture and appreciate my own European identity.

As I lacked knowledge about the history of this great land, let alone its people and culture, I challenged myself to learn as much as I could about the United States and its great heritage! As an avid reader, my English skills improved, and I was eager to read more and more historical literature. To become more familiar with my new language, I began to read about American culture and historical events. I soon learned about the early presidents, the duties of congress, and the justice system.

While studying ninth grade English Literature, I became interested in Shakespeare and particularly his play, *Julius Caesar*. I fondly remember taking the bus from school to the Folger Library near the Library of Congress and immersing myself in reading about the life and work of William Shakespeare—a totally new experience for me! I had never heard the English language in such a powerful way as it was for me reading his plays. As a result, my English vocabulary grew, and I began to feel more connected with my studies.

One very important aspect of my life was missing. While the Gardner family provided me with "so many things," I now realize that they did not personally nurture my spiritual life. Even though we attended church services at a small Episcopal church, as a family we did not engage in discussions about our faith. I did find some comfort in the Episcopalian worship rituals such as taking the sacraments and reciting the prayers which reminded me of my Catholic background. These moments brought back memories of my years with Maria when we faced our fears with prayer, and the times when I witnessed my faith among fellow DP refugees.

I am thankful that the Gardners provided opportunities for me to meet a group of Russian refugees who held worship services in a side chapel of the Washington National Cathedral. This wonderful group nurtured my faith in God and allowed me to share my background and talk of Ukrainian life. It was then that I met Galya. She was a beautiful girl from Russia, and we enjoyed sharing our common heritage as very close friends. Galya and her mother were also experiencing difficult transitions. They lived in a cramped attic of an American family as Galya's mother worked to care of their small children. They were like me—trying to adjust to new American life. The cheerful disposition that Galya's mother displayed every time I remember being with her inspired me to see my circumstances in a more positive light. I soon began to seek out opportunities to be with Galya and her mother as often as I could. We frequently enjoyed going on adventures within the city as we learned about familiar landmarks and interesting places such as museums, parks, and movie theaters.

One such memory I have is of Galya and I going to see the movie *Swan Lake* based on the ballet written by the famous Tchaikovsky. We must have seen that movie a dozen times!

Another adventure that comes to my mind was when we went on one of our many picnics with the other Russian refugees. One day in particular, Galya's mother joined us as we went with a young boy to a picnic where we would join other Russian refugees. As our luck would have it, there were fewer people at the picnic, and the small group dispersed earlier than we had planned. To make matters worse, the boy became interested in another young girl at the picnic, and he completely forgot about us! It did not take us long to realize that he and his "new girlfriend" had left us, and we were stranded! As a rain storm was approaching, we began to try to find our way back home. At first, there was a feeling of panic because we really did not know where we were in relationship to our homes. We walked to the closest highway and began to try to determine what direction to go. As we were on a hill, Gayla and I were able to look toward the DC area to recognize prominent landmarks that we knew from our previous outings. We felt somewhat of a relief knowing that we were oriented in a homeward bound direction. However, the rainstorm was advancing our way, and we knew that we needed to be proactive in finding someone to help us. As we walked along the highway, it began to rain harder with blowing wind. We soon realized that no one wanted to stop their car to pick up three rain soaked and soggy individuals. After walking for what it seemed like an hour, a kind stranger stopped his car and asked if he could help us. Because Gayla's mother did not speak much English, Gayla began to explain our plight. I thought of the Walter Reed Hospital which was not far from my home. I spoke up to tell the gentleman that if he could take us to the hospital, then we could walk home from there. It was then that I realized that I knew more about my home and surroundings than I thought I did. How empowering it was for me to know that I could use what little knowledge I had to find my way home. As we got closer to more familiar surroundings, I felt a sense of pride in myself for knowing that I *could* find my own way. I remember thinking back to my journeys with Maria and wondering if she ever felt lost. As a child, I always had faith that Maria knew where she was going and could find the right path for us. Maria was faith-filled and resourceful, and her example taught me to be resilient.

Upon arrival at the Walter Reed Hospital, and we expressed our thanks to the kind man for his graciousness to provide us transportation. After our walk back to my house on Van Buren Street, I invited Gayla and her mother into the house for some hot tea to warm ourselves. I had observed Margaret many times hosting guests and serving them using her beautiful china teacups. How good it felt to feel that *I could invite my friends* and serve them in the comfort of *my* home! I had never had a feeling such as this! However, my elation soon came to an end when I clumsily dropped the sugar bowl as I was offering Gayla's mother a sugar cube for her drink. The bowl broke into several pieces, and I was gripped with fear as to what my mother would say. To my surprise, as she came into the room, she did not seem to be upset over the loss of her lovely sugar bowl that matched her china. She praised me for welcoming my friends and preparing tea for them. It was later when Gayla and her mother left that I apologized to my mother for breaking her beautiful bowl. I was impressed with how little the broken china meant to her, but how proud she was of me that I tried to make my friends feel welcome in *our* home.

However, my sweet friendship with Galya was all too soon to be interrupted.

*I know what it is to be in need, and I know what it is to have plenty. I have learned the secret of being content in any and every situation, whether well fed or hungry, whether living in plenty or in want, I can do everything through him who gives me strength. (Philippians 4:12–13, NIV)*

# Finding My Way

The next year my father retired from the US Army and took a job in his native California as a doctor for the San Diego Health Department. We moved to San Diego, and my parents located a home in a wealthy neighborhood. Nonna enrolled in San Diego State College, and I attended Point Loma High School. As I entered a new school setting, I so much wanted to be accepted by my new peers and belong to the "Tre Jolie" club—meaning "beautiful" in French—as *all* the popular girls were members. In an effort to "join the crowd," I enrolled in dancing lessons. Nonna was already an accomplished dancer, and my parents wanted me to have the same opportunity. I will never forget when I received my first "tap shoes." Not only did they make the clicking sounds as I walked across hard wood floors, they were also black and shiny and tied with a bow. My greatest accomplishment was learning to do "shuffle, ball, change." As my arms and hands were flailing in the air, and my feet were moving to the tapping rhythm, I felt a new awareness of my body.

Of course, my mother declared that there was to be no tap dancing on her beautiful hardwood floors, so outside I went down the concrete driveway and into the street! I was so impressed with the clicking tap sounds coming from my feet, that I embellished my movements with leaps and twirls. Every tap movement seemed to make its own music. As enamored as I was with my new found talent, the neighbors were not, especially the elderly couple next door who shared the common ally driveway with us! It seemed that I was always disturbing them as they were trying to take their mid-afternoon naps. Dancing was a liberating feeling for me as it brought back the fond memories of first learning to dance with my refugee friends at the DP Camp in Bad Aibling. However, my new reality was that my attempts to learn the precise dance steps did not seem to impress my new girlfriends. Making friends was terribly awkward and difficult for me as I felt that I was always on the "outside looking in."

Therefore, I thrust myself into my academic studies because I knew I had a tremendous desire for learning and knowledge, especially of history. I also wanted to please my parents and meet their high expectations for me to achieve. I so much wanted their approval, and I soon realized that excelling in the academic arena would make them proud.

In my continued efforts to gain my father's attention, I eagerly volunteered to accompany him on some of his various trips to outlying clinics in the San Diego area. He did not make clinic visits very often, but when the occasion presented itself, I was enthusiastic about spending time with him. I think he seemed pleased that I was taking an interest in his work. Because Nonna was then completing her college work, I had more opportunities to be alone with Leon and engage in conversation in the car that over time bonded us. Having my father all to myself was very comforting and reassuring to me that I had his undivided attention.

I remember one such trip when we went to Ocean Beach located north of San Diego. My father was going to provide supervision in a clinic there that was staffed by nurses. It surprised me to observe how "in control" my father seemed to be—in the most caring way. I could see his compassion and concerned demeanor for some of the family members of Marines who came from the nearby military base, Camp Pendleton. Seeing my father in his "doctor" role helped me to know him on another level than what I had observed him to be in our home environment. At home, it was my mother who seemed to be the one "in control," and my father appeared to me to be more passive and relaxed. Watching him in the clinic as he talked in a consoling way to a distraught mother worried about her young ill son, revealed a side of him that I had not seen before. I remember feeling how fortunate I was to have such a man as him for my father. As time went on, I soon began to share experiences with my father that became treasured memories.

I realized that Leon and I had much in common. He loved the opera and camping, both interests that I also eagerly enjoyed. As we camped in many local areas in Baja, California, in the desert and the mountains north of Los Angeles, Leon shared his love for observing birds in their natural habitats. Baja offered beautiful vistas of the ocean and the mountains. I think my father loved this area so much for its peaceful silence and solitude. However, when hiking and camping in this area, one had to be very careful as it was known that bandits were dangers that unsuspecting campers might encounter. I remember one such occasion when my father and I were camping below Ensenada about thirty-five miles from Tijuana, Mexico, when we were awakened by some rustling noises outside our tent. We saw two dark figures approaching. My father immediately got his revolver which he always carried with him while camping in that area. He discharged two shots into the air to let our intruders know that we were not defenseless. The individuals immediately turned and ran disappearing into the rugged terrain. I was completely shocked to see my father's reaction of deliberate and aggressive behavior toward these individuals. It seemed so out of character for him. While I was not fearful for our safety in this situation, I had flashback memories of my childhood when Maria and I were presented with similar circumstances where I was afraid. Maria, of course had no gun, but we always managed to survive unwelcomed visitors.

This camping experience was haunting to me as I perceived our campsite to be in a beautiful peaceful place where I truly did not feel threatened. However, when I was in war-torn Europe with all the bombings and destruction, soldiers carrying large rifles, and the desperate expressions of fear on peoples' faces as we all felt terrible danger around us, we never seemed to feel the need for a gun's protection. I began to wonder why my father thought the use of a gun was necessary. Perhaps I was still emotionally a young child in my naïve thinking and so trusting. Or…had I now experienced a new situation, much different than war, where my father was my protector and prepared to keep me from individuals who might pose a threat to our safety? I now realized that there was someone in my life who was there to protect and keep me safe from harm.

On our way home from camping near Ensenada, we saw a Mexican man walking in the direction toward Tijuana. Seeing this individual prompted me to ask my father if he would be willing to offer this man a ride with us since we were also going in his direction. I did this because I thought it might be interesting to "practice" my Spanish with a "real Mexican." My father was agreeable to the idea, and he stopped the car and invited the man to share a ride with us. He seemed to me to be an elderly man who was appreciative to lighten his journey. I immediately began reciting a lesson from my second year of Spanish:

"El burro es un animal muy importante,
El hombre pobre usa el burro.

El hombre rico no usa el burro;
Usa un automobile."

The Mexican man looked at me like he didn't know what to make of "this crazy American" who was trying to speak Spanish with a Russian accent! I truly hope that he was not offended, as my efforts to impress him were real. I wanted to try to relate to him by making an effort to speak "proper" Spanish. However, I realized that my intentions for friendly communication embarrassingly fell short as he was shaking his head with a bewildered look on his face! As we arrived in Tijuana, our passenger was grateful to finally be at his destination. Perhaps he was weary of my constant "Spanish chatter!"

When we left Tijuana, and approaching the border from Mexico into the United States, my father did not want to wait in the long line for our passports to be checked by the border guards. His impatience with the border control got the best of him as he devised a *plan*. His plan unfolded as he began to tell me about his missionary parents who were originally from the state of Massachusetts. Therefore, he decided to claim Massachusetts as his birth state even though he was born in China. I, however, with my heavy European accent, was a bit of a problem for him to explain to the border guards. Therefore, to remedy this dilemma, Leon asked me to pronounce the name of each state in the Union. I thought this was a strange request, but I did as my father asked as I named each state that I knew. My father just shook his head until I said, *"Ohio!"*

Leon immediately exclaimed, "That's it! You will tell the guard that you were born in Ohio!" My father then instructed me that when the border officer asked me personally where I was born, I was to clearly and proudly pronounce, "O-hi-o!" I was completely bewildered by his plan for I knew absolutely nothing about the great state of Ohio except a vague knowledge of its location. I had some intimidating past experiences with guards at border crossings in the Ukraine, Poland, and Germany, and I knew how the guards during the war were very vigilant regarding refugee documents. I truly did not think my father's scheme was a good one. However, I trusted him to make his plan work as we approached the border officials. To my amazement, the border guards let me pass, and my father and I had a good laugh all the way back to San Diego!

As our first year in San Diego progressed, so did my relationship with Nonna. While she was now "out of the home" living the college life, we both benefited from the distance we now had. Nonna began to recognize my intense interest in history, and she was eager to share with me a lecture on Latin America by one of her favorite and most interesting professors. I remember how excited I was when she invited me to go with her to one of her classes at San Diego State College. The professor was lecturing on Bolivia and its development. He talked about the people, culture, and economics which promoted my thinking about the Latin American countries. I realized that I now wanted to become more fluent in the Spanish language. This experience ignited a fire in me to go to college and learn more. Little did Nonna know how much that day with her meant to me. For the first time, we actually engaged in mutual discussion about her professor and what she was learning and how inspired she was to complete her studies. I so much appreciated her interest in me and sharing her knowledge.

The following Christmas, 1951, my friend Michael Kuzma was on holiday leave from his responsibilities in the US Air Force, and he came to visit me in my new California home. Reunited now, we both had matured, and our relationship was beginning to take a turn for us to begin thinking about our future. While my actual age was eighteen, my school peers and parents regarded me as being just sixteen. In my mind, I was becoming an adult, but others considered me to be just a young adolescent. Michael was already about twenty years old, and I think he wanted me to marry him. I knew at that time I was not ready for marriage and possible children. I also knew that the Gardners would be terribly disappointed in me if I chose to marry Michael before I had completed my future education. If I had taken such actions, they would surely have refused to help me, not only financially but also emotionally. I felt I could not leave these parents as they provided me tremendous stability for the first time in my life. I feared that such a decision would cause them to no longer care for me and have me as a part of their family. I could not accept the idea of their possible rejection. My overwhelming feelings to please my parents and achieve a college education overpowered any other feelings that I might have of a *love* for Michael. As I look back to that time in my life, it is clear to me now that a decision to marry Michael would have been short-sighted, and that both of us were truly not ready to enter into a lifetime relationship. As a young woman, I trusted my "inner-voice"—as I now realize that God was once again leading me.

As it happened, Michael and I remained friends as each of us chose to go our different ways. Time passed, and we drifted apart. I have often wondered whatever happened to Michael Kuzma… I know he had such promise for great success in his life.

During my senior year in high school (1952–1953), I was naturalized as a United States citizen. This was a powerful moment for me as I stood before a large audience and my fellow "new citizens" to present a speech that I had written entitled, "I Speak for America." I wrote this speech as a result of a public speaking course that I was taking as an elective. This class gave me confidence to use my voice and express myself. As a European with a heavy accent derived from my childhood exposure to many different languages and dialects, I was terribly self-conscious and fearful of people not understanding me. My father encouraged me to bring forth my feelings and use my knowledge in the most articulate ways that I could. As I prepared my speech, my father was a willing listener, and we engaged in long talks about what I had learned from studying the history of our great nation. These conversations with Leon helped me to gain the confidence that I needed to formulate my ideas and put them down on paper. It had only been three years prior when I arrived in the United States knowing nothing of this great land, its history, and symbols of Liberty.

Now, I felt ready to deliver my speech which gave me a sense of enormous pride to be a United States citizen. Not only was this moment a life event that I will never forget, it was also a time when I felt that I could truly look toward a future. For the first time in my life, I was no longer living in the moment for day to day survival. I was now looking *forward* to a college education and beyond. I had plans for the future which the Gardners and my teachers helped me to realize and make possible for myself. I had never dreamed of "possibilities" before! Speaking before all the other individuals who joined me to become US citizens, I felt a huge sense of destiny and the resolve to make myself worthy of the freedoms this great nation offered me and others. Thanks be to God!

After my high school graduation, I attended San Diego State college now San Diego State University just as Nonna did for two years and then transferred to Pomona College (now Pomona University), one of the prestigious colleges in California and my parents' alma mater. As a twenty-two-year-old woman, I entered Pomona in the fall of 1955, and because of my interest to become more fluent in Spanish, I resided in the *Spanish House*. During that time, I met Ana Maria Kong, a lovely girl from Guatemala. We quickly became friends, and she invited me to meet her family and spend the summer at her home in Guatemala City. I was delighted to be totally immersed in a new culture, and I vividly remember spending hours in Ana Maria's father's library poring over his books and reading Spanish literature. This wonderful summer experience with my dear friend's family spurred my interest even more to become more proficient in Spanish. My time in Guatemala also opened my mind and heart to a different culture of people from an Indian heritage. This experience made me realize that I wanted to know even more about other Hispanic cultures around the world. Therefore, when I returned to Pomona College in the fall, I decided to work harder to become more fluent in their language.

Foreign languages seem to come natural for me, and I was able to acquire new vocabulary quickly. As a very young child thrust into varying populations of refugees speaking a variety of European languages and dialects, I quickly learned Ukrainian, Russian, Polish, German, and in the DP Camps, I acquired some English before I arrived in the United States. My fluency in Spanish was a natural progression.

Pomona College presented great challenges for me because my overall education background was still terribly lacking. By attending San Diego State prior to entering Pomona, I missed the early basic coursework that Pomona College had to offer. My parents' decision to first send me to San Diego State was with good intentions to keep me close by them and give me time to adjust to their family life. However, I found it extremely difficult to "play catch-up" to my past war experiences of neglected academics. This resulted in me not passing all my required coursework at Pomona, which I later made up to graduate late in August, 1957.

Upon graduation, majoring in History with a Spanish minor, I received an education certificate to teach secondary Spanish in the public schools. Teaching high school students presented many unexpected challenges for me. I failed miserably in the classroom. I guess I had too much emotional baggage to be a good teacher. I felt tremendous frustration with some of my young high school students who did not take advantage of their educational opportunities. They seemed to let their social life take priority over their learning. How could these children of privilege not recognize the value of learning? I had very little patience with them! I all too soon realized that I needed to rethink my idea of being a teacher. However, I have a great respect for the teaching profession, and I have fond memories of some of my past teachers and professors who greatly made an impact in my life. I remember two teachers at Pomoma College who nurtured my love of history and foreign languages. One professor who taught Russian culture helped me to appreciate my own Russian heritage. I finally felt validated and proud of where I had come from! It was Professor Stein teaching Russian language and Ancient History who challenged me to refine and sharpen my own Russian speech. For the first time, I learned the correct grammar and vocabulary of my own native language. This knowledge empowered me to be confident in expressing myself. It is interesting to recall that there were only three students in this Russian class because *what American student would want to learn Russian in the late 1950s!* Little did we understand that the Soviet Union was challenging our country in the Cold War as a major power in the world.

My love for reading led me to consider a possible career as a librarian. Before entering the University of Southern California (USC) in the coming summer (1959) to work toward a master's degree in library science, I decided to volunteer in a real library setting to determine if this was a profession that I would enjoy. In the spring, I began working at the Scripps Institute of Oceanography where the head librarian introduced me to a woman who analyzed and organized periodicals in the field of oceanography. She introduced me to working with documents written in German and Russian. This offered me a tremendous opportunity to use my languages skills as well as extend my own knowledge of a new science. My parents wisely encouraged me to live independently with a lady named Mrs. Leftwich who lived in a small home about a twenty-minute walk from Scripps. I have fond memories of my daily walks as I passed the lovely hills on one side and admired the magnificent views of the ocean on the other. It was hard to believe that these scenes of serenity and sparking beauty could turn into such fury when the warm weather changed to torrential rains and violent storms.

It was not long before I realized that my work at Scripps was enormously stimulating and challenging. I knew that library science would be a field where I could excel and find tremendous satisfaction. Thus, I completed my master's degree program from the University of Southern California within a year, in May of 1960. I was determined to use my knowledge of library science and my experience at Scripps to advance my dreams of a profession dealing with books. Ever since my early years as a small child in war-torn Europe, books provided a refuge and comfort for me. I fondly had recurring memories of sitting close to Maria nestled in her arms and listening to her read stories from some of the great Russian writers. Those days molded me intellectually and to a great extent, emotionally as well.

Even though I sorely lacked a formal education in my childhood as a refugee, I recognized how profoundly grateful I was to Leon and Margaret Gardner for their determination and constant vigilance to provide me with the highest educational opportunities possible. As a couple well into their years, they made a huge difference in my life, as well as in the lives of Jeannie and Nonna. For them to embrace the enormous responsibility of adopting three young adolescent girls and nurturing them to maturity remains deep in my heart of gratitude.

I wanted to apply my skills at the highest level. I will never forget the day when I was working in the USC periodical section looking for job opportunities in my field. My eye came upon a brochure promoting the hiring of special recruits at the Library of Congress. My mind immediately recalled my previous days in Washington, DC, and I immediately began to pursue the challenge to apply for a position there.

To my amazement, I received an acceptance letter from the special recruit program in early August, 1960. Of course, my parents were elated to realize that I would be returning to Washington, DC to work at the prestigious Library of Congress. My mother was especially excited because she had a wide circle of friends there whom she knew both professionally and socially. She was certain that her friends would be a support group for me to rely on when I needed them. I think she thought that I would seek out her contacts and embrace their social life style. However, I knew that I was not Margaret, and that I needed to find my own way to survive in a new professional culture. As I prayed for guidance, I began to feel prepared and excited to embrace whatever my new job offered me. I had faith that I could move forward.

*And we know that in all things God works for the good of those who love him, who have been called according to his purpose. (Romans 8:28, NIV)*

# Am I Living in a Circle?

During my first few weeks "on the job," there were numerous meetings with the heads of various departments and the seven newly hired recruits from all over the country. We received floods of communication and information about possible areas of interest and work. For about six months, I rotated among the many departments within the Library of Congress to determine what my specialty area might be. I expressed my interest in knowing more about the modern day Soviet Union and using my language skills. Therefore, I was assigned to the Aerospace Information Division. While the job did not require scientific knowledge (as in the Aerospace Research Department), my work primarily required a knowledge of the Russian language. This was very significant because I was reading and translating publications in various aspects of Russian research and technology. There were times when my job also focused on reading Russian books and manuals that were very trivial in nature; however, the US government wanted translations of any and all Russian documents as the United States was now in a tense Cold War and "Space Race" with the Soviet Union. Finally, I was beginning to understand that my Russian background and experiences were valuable assets to me and to my country. I realized how important it was to have a job that was gratifying and left me with a sense of purpose at the end of each day!

However, the two years I spent in Washington were lean ones for me, as to live in that city one needed money and position; and even though my job was important to the country, librarians were not well paid. I was lucky to find a small apartment two blocks from my office. Walking a distance to work was very enjoyable to me; for whenever I took a bus, I felt it depressing to see so many tired people coming home from their jobs. Walking gave me energy and calmness—an opportunity to pray and reflect on my day.

While my work was intellectually stimulating, I felt terribly isolated and alone on a very personal level. I realized that while there were a few of my mother's friends who had reached out to me, I found it difficult to relate to them. I knew that it was important for me to live my life independent of people who truly only related to my mother's generation. Many of Margaret's friends were very much older than me, and some were no longer living. I needed the feeling of true friendship. I experienced some very lonely times.

My lifeline was my reconnection with Bozhana and her mother, Mrs. Trost. I visited them very often and thrived on the feeling of having a close relationship to a mother figure once again. Mrs. Trost was always welcoming and seemed to truly be interested in making me feel *valued*. I needed this feeling of acceptance in my life. Even for a short time, my encounter with Bozhana and her mother filled a tremendous void of not having a family close by. While I was experiencing a personal life that seemed to *me* to lack purpose, I now realize how important that time was for me to reflect on *"where was I going from here?"*

In the late spring of 1962, I had an unsettled feeling and the desire to make a change. After attending a local job fair and learning about the opportunities for civilian librarians in the Special Services of the US Army, I began to focus on a plan. I wanted to use my knowledge of history, the Russian and German languages, as well as my degree in library science, to offer my gratitude to the US Army for helping me escape the aftermath of the war in Europe and for providing me the opportunity to begin a new life in the United States. I signed with the US Army as a civilian and was sent to Germany to work in the Army camps as a librarian with the equivalent rank of captain.

In November, 1962, my first assignment was in Augsburg, Germany, a very old historical city not far from Munich. My work focused on maintaining organization in the base libraries; first, at Army camps Sheridan Kaserne and Infantry Kaserne, both staffed by the German nationals. My role was to provide educational support to the soldiers by acquiring books and catalogs for them to learn more about Germany and its people and culture. Another aspect of my scope included educating the American soldiers regarding the current Cold War issues with the Soviet Union. At the time of my arrival, the Cuban Missile Crisis from October 16–28 was still very fresh on the minds of our troops. These young soldiers had just experienced a thirteen-day political and military stand-off between the United States and the Soviet Union. This happened when President John Kennedy told the American public in an October twenty-second television address that our US intelligence information indicated that there were Soviet nuclear missiles on the island of Cuba aimed toward the United States. President Kennedy revealed to the viewing audience that the United States Navy would blockade the waters around Cuba, and that he would order US military forces to prevent pending future Soviet shipments of missiles being delivered to Cuba. For this moment in time, all of our military installations around the world were on the highest alert. Among all the tension, our troops in Germany were especially concerned about any possible aggressive military action that might be taken from the Soviets occupying East Germany. Such an invasion would be devastating in Europe and another world war would be launched. The Cold War was upon our troops, and they waited for their orders...

On October twenty-eight, Khrushchev capitulated, and the Soviet ships bearing nuclear missiles turned away from the quarantine zones around Cuba. As a result of the intense communications between the two world leaders, John Kennedy and Nikita Khruschchev, the missile sites were dismantled, and the current missiles on the island of Cuba were returned to the Soviet Union.

While there was a huge sigh of "nervous relief" that a nuclear war had been diverted, our soldiers' interests in the Russian people heightened. As the base librarian, I worked very hard to access information materials and locate interesting speakers that our troops might appreciate and find to be enlightening. It was important to me to relate my own experiences and knowledge of the days since the Stalin regime. I felt it was critical for our soldiers to have some historical understanding of the Soviet citizens in the USSR under the current political leadership of Khrushchev. I knew that I was at the right place at the right time in my life. Therefore, I diligently planned seminars and discussion groups that focused on the Soviet people, their culture, their geography, and the current Soviet government policies and restrictions.

For the Army's recognition of *Library Month* in April of 1963, I wrote a booklet for the soldiers to help them appreciate some historical information about Augsburg and its beautiful buildings. A part of my writing focused on the Die Fuggerei built by a wealthy merchant named Jakob Fugger who lived in the fourteenth century. While working on my research, I found some interesting details about him. I learned that Jakob was concerned for his poor laborers and built them housing that consisted of small stone structures that provided bedrooms and basic living quarters. The workers entered each room from the street for them to come and go without disturbing other inhabitants.

This seemed to me to be a very progressive experiment in early social welfare. My intent in providing this and other similar information was to make the soldiers aware of historical social responsibility that originated in early Europe. It was disappointing to me that some of the young soldiers whom I worked with had very little interest in the local culture and history around them. They were totally absorbed in their own desires to return to the United States. While I understood their longing for homes and families, I was frustrated with their lack of interest to learn more about the wealth of history around them. How could they find purpose and meaning in their work, when they cared so little for the German people? This was something that I, too, had to realize for myself when I was trying to find my inner peace living in the United States. I learned that when I reached beyond *my* world and personal concerns and stretched myself to learn more about other cultures and people, I soon found meaning in my own mundane life.

While in Augsburg, I had the opportunity to travel and see the beautiful countryside. Being in the foothills of the German Alps, I learned how to snow ski. This was a highly unlikely accomplishment for a California transplant! I loved the sport and took every chance I had to go to the nearby slopes. The US Army maintained two recreation resorts for its soldiers—one at Garmisch-Partenkirchen and Berchtesgaden. This area was close to the location of Adolf Hiltler's Kehlsteinhaus (Eagle's Nest), a retreat hideaway presented to him as a gift from the Nazi Party for his fiftieth birthday. It has been said that Hitler rarely came to Eagle's Nest as he was terrified of heights and did not trust the elevator!

I recall one beautiful bright sunny day when I saw a group of four-and five-year-old children who were skiing down the slopes without the slightest trace of fear. Their American families were on holiday and enjoying time off from their duties at the Army base. The expressions on some of the mothers' faces showed their anxieties for the safety of their young ones. However, the children were delighted and joyful as they raced down the hills. Watching these fearless youngsters caused me to reflect upon my own very young years with Maria when I, too, seemed to know little of fear. It is amazing how resilient young children are in their own environments and have a feeling of well-being. Children seem to be able to feel *goodness* and freedom when in reality their surroundings are perilous situations with possible harm. Watching those children that day, helped me to realize how far I had come since my early turbulent years, and that I had *survived* places of danger and managed to overcome so many obstacles. There was no fear in me now!

My work in the lovely old city of Augsburg brought me to a special place that I could have never imagined as a young sixteen-year-old refugee in 1949. Now, in 1963, I returned to this place as a twenty-nine-year-old educated woman of faith for I knew Jesus Christ, and that God had a plan for me to be in Germany again. His plan for my future began to reveal itself on the day when I was carrying a heavy load of books and walking across the courtyard in the Infantry Kaserne. I saw a young private walking in my direction, and outranking him, I quickly commanded, "*Soldier, carry my books!*" which he obediently did!

I soon began to take more notice of Private Graham Nichols with his broad smile and quick wit. At first, he was a little intimidated by me perhaps since I was a captain; however, it was not long before he gathered the courage to ask me to go see a movie on base, *The Requiem for a Heavyweight.* I did not think it was much of a movie; but Graham, being a sports fan, thoroughly enjoyed it!

What impressed me about Graham was that he was determined to learn the German language and voluntarily enrolled in German language classes at Infantry Kaserne. He enjoyed mingling among the German people in the town and surrounding areas to "try out" his new German vocabulary and conversational phrases. He felt so accomplished when he could engage in a brief conversation with a native German and feel that he had made a real connection with someone whom he did not know. Our friendship grew as we continued to date on and off the Army base, enjoying each other's company.

An unexpected surprise for me was a letter that I received from Bozhana, my dearest friend in Washington, DC, who was planning a visit to spend time with her family in Slovenia. In her correspondence, she asked me if I could meet her in Munich at the airport where she was to arrive about ten or eleven o'clock in the morning. I was elated as I planned my trip to greet her! I left Augsburg by train in time to be at the Munich airport. However, upon arrival at the airport, I received news that Bozhana's flight would be late. My *short* wait became a *long* wait as there were repeated announcements of her airplane being delayed into the night. This went on for more than twelve hours! Her plane finally arrived safely around one o'clock the next morning! Both of us were overjoyed to finally see each other again. However, we were very tired and a bit concerned as to how we would get a train back to Augsburg at such a late hour. We found a taxi and asked the driver to take us to the Munich train station, only to discover when we arrived that the last train for Augsburg had already left. Feeling a bit desperate, we both pooled what money we had between us and asked the driver to take us to our destination in Augsburg where we arrived totally exhausted and very broke!

Nevertheless, we thoroughly enjoyed the next few days we had together reminiscing and traveling in the local countryside, including a brief trip to Innsbruck, a lovely mountain resort town in the Austrian Alps. I was determined to introduce my new love of skiing to Bozhana, so we journeyed to Garmisch, where she soon learned about the challenges of standing on slippery slopes with skis on her feet and her bottom quickly meeting the ground! Our laughter was exuberant and joyous as we enjoyed our time together. We truly were friends for a lifetime!

While in Augsburg, Bozhana stayed with me in my small apartment, and she expressed interest in my work on the base, as well as meeting my friends. Of course, I was eager for her to meet Graham. I recall one evening when he came to visit and brought with him all the ingredients and food to prepare a dinner for us. I knew Graham liked to cook, but his overture to prepare a complete meal for the three of us was quite surprising. He encouraged Bozhana and me to leave the apartment while he was preparing his "feast." He assured us that his preparations would take a lot of time, so he urged me to take Bozhana sightseeing. I decided to take Bozhana to see some of the beautiful churches in Augsburg. As we explored several of the amazing sites and marveled at the beautiful historical structures, we also found ourselves immersed in some of the quaint little shops.

Time began to pass more quickly than we had anticipated, so when we finally arrived back at the apartment, to our dismay, Graham's lovely meal was *cold!* I felt terrible about not judging our time better, but Graham was very forgiving, and he quickly rewarmed the entire meal for us all to enjoy. Once again, I was impressed with his patience and his willingness to make Bozhana feel welcome.

After serving in Augsburg for about a year, I received a new assignment to work in Munich at the US Army Hospital library and in Bad Aibling library. How very strange it was to return to a place where my future in 1949 had been so perilous and uncertain in a DP Camp! I realized then that my return to Bad Aibling, Germany, brought me full circle in a most profound way that I would *never* have dreamed to happen.

> *Trust in the Lord with all your heart and lean not on your own understanding; in all your ways acknowledge him, and he will make your paths straight. (Proverbs 3:5–6, NIV)*

# A Changing World

In the early 1960's all of Europe was still feeling the aftermath of World War II and the current Cold War. The German people were continuing their efforts to recover from the mass destruction, and there was still huge construction going on in the major cities. While I was working in Munich on my new assignment, I had recurring flashbacks of riding on a train in 1949 seeing Munich in ruins of rubble and destruction. Now, to my amazement, it was becoming a modern city. It seemed liked the world that I once knew was changing. Little did I know that there were shockwaves on the horizon...

I will never forget November 23, 1963, when I was in my fifth floor apartment getting ready to go to the Munich Hospital library. At that time, my work hours were from 1:00 p.m. to 9:00 p.m. to accommodate soldiers in the library after their regular daily duty hours. As I was preparing to leave my apartment, I heard unfamiliar noises coming from outside. Looking out one of my windows, I saw soldiers congregating below in an area near my apartment building. There was erratic commotion among the soldiers below; some were shouting and seemingly agitated. Others were randomly seated on the ground with their heads in their hands. I immediately knew that there was something terribly wrong.

I quickly ran down the five flights of steps into the courtyard when a young soldier ran up to me with tears streaming down his face, "They have killed my President!" I was stunned!

My body felt limp and quivery as I sought out soldiers to give me information. It was then that I learned that President John F. Kennedy was assassinated in Dallas, Texas. With all the commotion, I was numb and could hardly believe what I was hearing! The anguished and tear-soaked faces of our young soldiers that day—I will never forget. Yes, indeed, the world had changed…

After several months had passed, I had hopes of traveling back to see the reconstruction progress in Berlin. However, the Communist Soviet Union divided the city in 1961 by "the Wall" that separated East and West. It was heavily fortified by border guards, and many people in East Berlin lost their lives trying to flee into West Berlin. The city was an isolated enclave and political tensions remained volatile. Therefore, the US Army officials told me that I could not go back to Berlin unless I could pass as an American wearing a Special Services uniform. I was strongly advised *not* to go into Berlin because of my Russian accent. The Soviets considered "once a Russian, always a Russian," and I was warned that as an educated young woman that I could possibly be returned to my homeland in the Soviet Union. This disappointed me greatly as I wanted to see the "rebuilt" Berlin after the ruins of World War II. I also had lingering feelings of possibly locating and reuniting with my dear Tante Anna in Berlin as well. Recognizing that all of this was impossible for me, I grieved for not being able to see her again. I could not help but wonder that she might still be alive. I knew that Tante Anna would be so proud of me, and that we would rejoice in our reunion. So very sad…however, I soon realized that I had not come this far to return to past memories, but that I needed to focus on my new future.

Graham was now more important to me than ever. While he was still stationed in Augsburg, and I was in Munich, we overcame the challenge of the distance between us. Graham took every opportunity to take the train from Augsburg to Munich whenever he was granted leave from his Sergeant. We enjoyed traveling around Munich and surrounding cities and villages—even as far as Paris, Rome, and Vienna. God was moving in our lives as we found a trusting friendship where we both had felt past loneliness and realized that we had much in common. It was not long before we were very much in love, and I knew our relationship was the best thing that I could have ever imagined in my life!

Graham and I were married *twice* on March 24, 1964! We had a civil ceremony in Munich at the German Standesamt, a government office and then returned to the US Army base for a second marriage ceremony with friends attending in the Army Hospital Chapel. Our wedding trip from Germany to Switzerland and on to Venice was a dream come true for both of us!

Upon our return to the United States in 1964, Graham completed his education and received his master's degree from the University of North Carolina in Chapel Hill where I was a librarian in the Wilson Library on campus. As Graham and I established "our home" together, we were blessed with a precious son, Ernest, born in 1965. During the following years, Leon and Margaret remained in California, and as always, they continued their loving support and interest in my life—very happy to be grandparents! Leon died in 1982, and Margaret passed a year later. After our son graduated from college, we soon welcomed our lovely daughter-in-law, Libby, who gave us two wonderful grandchildren, Aaron and Justin.

North Carolina is our home with a vibrant church family and dear friends. As Charles Kuralt, a famous North Carolina writer and journalist, referred to our state as the "goodliest land," I know this to be true.

Now and forever, I thank God for bringing me to my advanced age and for his many blessings in my life! I have found *Home*!

> *Teach us to number our days aright, that we may gain a heart of wisdom. (Psalm 90:12, NIV)*

# Reflection

I come from many religious perspectives—Russian Orthodox, Catholic, Baptist, Episcopal, and Methodist. I believe that none of the traditional formal structures of worship supersede the personal religious experience that one has when engaged in personal prayer and conversation with God. I had to find this inner peace and experience it for myself. My story is a testimony of an evolving life-long process of finding my deep love of God and his son, Jesus. I know that he has always been with me from by birth, and when I was a homeless child and as an adult seeking guidance. I was never alone.

When I think on all my memories of situations where I was desperate to survive and clearly in profound danger, I *now* know that God was working through *specific* persons to bring me to where I am today—my birth parents, Ninna Fidler and Anatolii Sergeevich Wolkovich; my Godmother, Maria; Tante Anna; the American Army officer in Berlin; the Russian Orthodox priest; Dr. Leon and Margaret Gardner; my husband, Graham; and many others since. Thanks be to God for all these individuals!!

As I reflect on my early life and the circumstances that I faced, my memories are powerful, real, and vivid, as though they happened to my best friend whom I know very, very well. I marvel at how my life unfolded when so many of my experiences could have gone so wrong!

Inna Wolkovich Gardner Nichols
2018

*For I know the plans I have for you, declares the Lord, plans to prosper you and not to harm you, plans to give you hope and a future. (Jeremiah 29:11, NIV)*

1946
Inna (age 13) after Maria died

1947
Fourth Grade all female class in Berlin
(Inna is the third child from the right on the front row)

1947
Tante Anna and Inna (age 14)

1948
Tante Anna, Inna (age 14), and a Jewish friend
saying "Good-bye" at the Merienfelde Refugee
Transfer Camp outside of Berlin

1948
Inna and Maria Kabanoff, a Baptist woman who
witnessed her faith to Inna at the Merienfelde Camp

1948
Refugee friends (The girl on Inna's right was very artistic
and wanted to go to the U.S. to become a clothes designer.)

1948

Christmas pageant at the Bad Aibling Camp Michael Kuzma is St. Nicholas with Inna on his left and Jadwiga on his right, both playing the roles as angels. The third girl on Michael's right is Katrina, a Ukrainian, who was his girlfriend for a time and later went to Australia.

1949

English class at the Bad Aibling D.P. Camp The boy on the left is Jewish, and the other students are Ukrainian. Inna and Jawigna are seated on the far-right side.

1949
Inna and her first friend, Jadwiga Botcharenok,
at the Bad Aibling Camp (ages 16).

1949
Refugees arriving in New York City.
(Inna second from the right)

1950
Inna (on the left) with her adopted family, Dr. Leon
Gardner, Mrs. Margaret Gardner, and Nonna

1950
Inna and Nonna wearing their native dresses
with their adopted sister, Jeannie

1950
Inna, Galya, and a friend from church
enjoying American popsicles.

1951
Michael Kuzma in his U.S. Air Force uniform

1953
High School Graduation

1957
Pomona College Graduation

1963
Inna leading a Bad Aibling Special
Services Library presentation

Graham, Inna, and their son, Ernest

Ernest and Libby and their sons, Aaron and Justin

Inna and Graham vacationing in the
North Carolina mountains.

# Timeline of Inna's Early Life in Context with Specific Pre-and Post- WWII Historical Events

| Year | Inna | History |
|------|------|---------|
| 1928 | Inna's father, an ardent Bolshevik, opposed Josef Stalin's regime. | Josef Stalin emerged as the dictator of the Soviet Union. |
| 1933 | August 11, 1933, Inna is born in Kharkiv in eastern Ukraine. | January 30—Rising to power, Adolf Hitler is appointed chancellor of Germany. |
| 1934 | Inna lives with her parents in Kiev, Ukraine. | August—Hitler becomes Fuhrer and Supreme Commander of Germany. |
| 1935 | Inna's father is imprisoned as a result of his Leninist writings. | September—Hitler declared the Jews lose full German citizenship and enforced harsh restrictions upon them. |
| 1936 | Stalin sentences Inna's father to a hard labor camp in Siberia. Suffering from severe depression, Inna's mother gives young Inna to Maria. | Hitler used the Berlin Olympic games to promote his Aryan ideals. March 7—Hitler ignores the Versailles Treaty of 1919 and sends troops to reoccupy the Rhineland. |
| 1939 | Inna lives with Maria and Artemiy in Kiev, Ukraine. In the early winter, they are relocated to a temporary apartment west of Kiev. | September 1—The war began when German Forces invaded Poland. September 3—War in Europe escalates as Great Britain and France declared war on Germany. September 17—Soviet Union invades Poland. September 7–29—Germany and Soviet Union divide Poland between them. |
| 1941 | Inna lives with Maria and Artemiy in Kiev, Ukraine. | September 16–19—German army invades and takes Kiev. Kharkov, Poland is occupied by Germans. Germany begins extermination of Jews in eastern Europe. |
| 1942 | Artemiy dies in March. Maria and Inna journey into the foothills of the Carpathian Mountains in Poland finding refuge with Maria's sister. | December 4—German army comes within 15 miles of Moscow. December 6—German armies withdraw and are defeated outside of Moscow. |

| | | |
|---|---|---|
| 1943 | October—Maria and Inna flee into Krakow to escape from the Russian advancements. | January—German army fails to take Stalingrad. September 14—Soviet armies moving to take back Kiev. September 27—German army begins to withdraw in Ukraine and advance into Poland. |
| 1944 | In the spring Maria and Inna make their way into Silesia, Germany. In the summer, Maria and Inna find meager housing near Konrad in Berlin. | November 18—The US and Great Britain began air aggression on Berlin with British planes bombing at night and the US Air Force bombing by day. |
| 1945 | Maria's health is deteriorating. Living conditions are extremely difficult due to the cold winter. Food is very scarce. Berliners accepted their defeat as the Russian army invaded and occupied Berlin. In the summer after Maria's death, Inna lives with Anna Glinka in her small apartment. By September, living conditions were horribly extreme as Berliners were experiencing a severe food shortage. | January 17—Soviet army occupies Warsaw, Poland, and moving toward Berlin. April 1—Stalin tells his armies that the Soviets will "take Berlin before the Allies do." April 12—US President Roosevelt dies. April 25—Soviet army circles Berlin. April 26—First Soviet bombs hit the Chancellery in Berlin. April 30—Hitler commits suicide. May 1—The Red Army raised a Soviet flag over the Reichstag building's entrance. May 2—Berlin surrenders. May 7/8—Germans surrendered unconditionally to the Allies |

| | | |
|---|---|---|
| 1946 | Inna and Anna endured extreme cold with very little heat during the winter months. They continued to experience dire hunger and harsh living conditions along with thousands of Berliners. | March—Tensions between US and Soviet Union mount and a divided Berlin and Europe results. The Soviets occupy East Berlin and East Germany to impose harsh Soviet law.<br><br>June—The US Marshall Plan provides aid to West Berlin.<br>The Soviet Union creates a blockade around Berlin to force the US, Great Britain, and France out of the western half of Berlin. |
| 1947 | Inna and Anna continue to experience severe hunger and cold. | The Berlin Blockade and Airlift begins. |
| 1948 | In February Inna encounters danger with the Russian authorities who seek to return her to the Soviet Union.<br><br>Inna escapes to a temporary DP Camp in Marienfelde.<br><br>In June, Inna is transferred to DP Camp of Aglaterhausen, near Heidelburg, Germany. | The occupying Allied authorities work to send refugees back to their homelands. |
| 1949 | Inna is transferred to the DP Camp in Bad Aibling.<br>November—Inna arrives in New York City in America. | Soviet Union tests their first atomic weapon; the nuclear arms race and the Cold War begins. |
| 1950 | In February, Inna was adopted by Dr. Leon and Mrs. Margaret Gardner in Washington, D.C. Inna's "new" parents enrolled her in the ninth grade at Paul Junior High School. | East Germany and West Germany are highly restricted areas. |
| 1951 | Dr. Gardner retired and the family moved to San Diego, California. Inna attended Point Loma High School. | The Soviet government seals the East-West borders of Germany. |
| 1953 | Inna became a US citizen and enrolled in San Diego State College. | Joseph Stalin died on March 5. Nikita Khrushchev gains power within the Communist Party as a successor. |
| 1955 | Inna transfers to Pomona College. | Cold War continues to escalate. |
| 1957 | In August, Inna graduated with a degree in History with a minor in Spanish. She began teaching high school students. | On October 4, the Soviet Union launched Sputnik 1, the first artificial earth satellite. The Space Race begins. |

| 1958 | Inna worked at Scripps Institute of Oceanography and began her graduate studies at the University of Southern California. | In March, after a Communist Party power struggle, Khrushchev became the Premier of the Soviet Union during the height of the Cold War. |
|------|------|------|
| 1960 | After Inna earned her master's degree in library science, she returned to Washington, DC, to work as a special recruit at the Library of Congress. | Tensions between USSR and the US escalate. |
| 1961 | Inna's work at the Library of Congress focused on translating Russian documents. | The Berlin Wall was erected and heavily fortified by border guards.<br><br>On April 12, Soviet cosmonaut, Yuri Gagarin, was the first man to orbit the earth in his spacecraft, "Vostok 1."<br><br>On May 15, Alan Shepard was the first American in space aboard his Mercury spacecraft "Freedom 7" on a suborbital flight. |
| 1962 | Inna signed as a civilian with the Special Services of the US Army to serve in Augsburg, Germany, at Army Camps Sheridn Kaserne and Infantry Kaserne. | February 20, John Glenn was the first American astronaut to orbit the earth in his aircraft, *Friendship 7.* The US and USSR were in a race to the moon.<br><br>October 16–28, the Cuban Missile Crisis was a confrontation that brought the US and the USSR close to war over the US intelligence reports indicating Soviet nuclear missiles in Cuba aimed at the US mainland. |
| 1963 | Inna was transferred to work in Munich at the US Army Hospital and in Bad Aibling. | June 26—US President, John Kennedy, visits Berlin and gives his "Ich bin ein Berliner" speech denouncing the Wall and declaring support for all Berliners.<br><br>November 22—President John Kennedy was assassinated in Dallas, Texas. |
| 1964 | On March 24, Inna married Graham Nichols. Later that year, they returned to the US to make their home in North Carolina. | It was not until November 1989 when the Berlin Wall falls, and east Germans were freed. |

# Questions for Individual or Group Reflections

When individuals come together to share their responses to a book that they have all read, it can be a powerful experience. A "book talk" group offers opportunities for readers to not only share their opinions and reflections about the story, but it also opens the door for individuals to relate their own stories. Sharing personal stories can generate connections for individuals to better understand each other and themselves. I found this to be true as I listened to Inna share her many stories with me. The connection I made with Inna deepened my faith and understanding of God's mercy and grace.

I am introducing the opportunity for the readers of *Searching for Home* to come together to relate their reflections about some of the lifetime stories Inna shared in my book. I have provided a few "springboard" questions that might help stimulate thoughts on what spoke to you the most. My hope is that you may relate the scripture at the end of each chapter to find the blessings that God promises.

Alice F. Hagaman

In the Beginning

Inna was born into a world of pending chaos. Her parents' marriage and their lives were destroyed.

1.  Do you know of family situations when individuals are torn apart?
2.  Ninna gave Inna to a woman named Maria. Have you or someone you know experienced crisis circumstances that resulted in decisions that affected both parents and their children?

> *Though my father and mother forsake me,*
> *The Lord will receive me.*
> *(Psalm 27:10, NIV)*

Going Forward

Inna was receiving mixed messages from some people whom she encountered.

1.  What impact did some of these encounters have on Inna?
2.  Have you experienced mixed messages and how did you resolve them?
3.  Inna forgave her mother. Have you experienced finding forgiveness?

> *A father to the fatherless...*
> *Is God in his holy dwelling.*
> *(Psalm 68:5, NIV)*

## Loss

Inna and Maria felt loss on many levels. As a young child, Inna observed and experienced the terror and horrors of war, destitution, and profound loss. She saw various people who demonstrated troubling behaviors as well as generous behaviors.

1.  Have you observed "troubling behaviors" when some people are experiencing highly stressful situations?
2.  Have you known people to show caring and compassionate behaviors toward others as they are experiencing their own difficult times of loss?

*Search me, O Lord, and know my heart;*
*test me and know my anxious thoughts.*
*(Psalm 139: 23, NIV)*

## Poland

Inna came to realize the presence of God in her life. She also realized that Maria was vital to her survival and feared separation from Maria.

1.  How did Inna's faith in God begin to evolve? Can you remember a time when you felt that you needed God in your life?
2.  Have you ever experienced a feeling of abandonment?

*I have told you these things, so that in me you may have peace.*
*In this world you will have trouble. But take heart!*
*I have overcome the world.*
*(John 16:33, NIV)*

Among the Ashes

Inna and Maria arrived in Berlin amid the worst time during the war (the day and night bombings). Their survival to stay alive was in great peril.

1. How did Inna cope with her fears?
2. Have you ever created routines or habits to help you cope with a fear or anxiety?

> *By day the Lord directs his love,*
> *at night his song is with me -*
> *a prayer to the God of my life.*
> *(Psalm 42:8, NIV)*

Critical Decisions

Tragedy and loss once again comes to Inna's young life in powerful ways.

1. How did Inna deal with her grief?
2. What do you think Inna meant when she said, "What an unlikely web of individuals God brought together!!"?
3. How did decisions made by critical people in Inna's life impact her future?
4. Can you relate to the power of decisions made by others that influenced your life?

> *Why are you downcast, O my soul?*
> *Why so disturbed within me?*
> *Put your hope in God,*
> *for I will yet praise him,*
> *my Savior and my God.*
> *(Psalm 42:5, NIV)*

## New Beginnings

Living in a Displaced Persons (D.P.) Camp was a whole new experience for Inna. At the age of 14, she truly was on her own without Maria and Tante Anna in her life. However, she knew she was not alone…

1. What unexpected "doors" opened for Inna?
2. Have you experienced a time when God seemed to put people in your path to help you find your way?

*Though I walk in the midst of trouble,*
*you preserve my life;*
*you stretch out your hand against the anger of my foes,*
*with your right hand you save me.*
*(Psalm 138:7, NIV)*

## Welcome to Another World!

When Inna arrived in the United States she was surprised to see "two different worlds—one for the rich, and one for the abandoned and neglected".

1. What were some of the conflicting realities that Inna experienced when she first arrived in America?
2. Have you or someone you know had a vision of what a place or a situation might be like; and then you had a disappointing or unexpected revelation?

*The Lord will fulfill his purpose for me;*
*Your love, O Lord, endures forever—*
*do not abandon the works of your hands.*
*(Psalm 138:8, NIV)*

A New Life with New Challenges

Inna was adopted by a prominent couple living in Washington, D.C. As an immigrant, Inna was thrusted into a different kind of culture where she daily found it difficult to survive.

1. What was Inna's reaction to the "abundance" of her American life?
2. For one who had previously experienced life with very few material things, why was it so difficult for Inna to accept and be happy with her new found "wealth"?

*Be strong and courageous.*
*Do not be afraid...*
*for the Lord your God goes with you;*
*he will never leave you nor forsake you.*
*(Deuteronomy 31:6)*

### Will I Ever Fit In?

Inna was immersed into a social and school environment where she felt that she could not cope.

1. What decisions did she make to "fit in"?
2. How did other people impact Inna's life? How did their actions make a difference?

> *I know what it is to be in need,*
> *and I know what it is to have plenty.*
> *I have learned the secret*
> *of being content in any and every situation,*
> *whether well fed or hungry,*
> *whether living in plenty or in want,*
> *I can do everything through him*
> *who gives me strength.*
> *(Philippians 4:12–13, NIV)*

### Finding My Way

Inna experiences another huge transition in her life. However, change was not all bad…

1. What people or events helped Inna to find herself?
2. How did decisions you made, or the experiences and relationships you had in your life change your direction?

> *And we know that in all things God works*
> *for the good of those who love him,*
> *who have been called according to his purpose.*
> *(Romans 8:28, NIV)*

Am I Living in a Circle?

New employment at the Library of Congress brought Inna back to Washington, DC. Two years later when she made the decision to work as a civilian librarian for the United States Army, Inna was assigned to an Army base in Augsburg, Germany.

1. Have you ever thought that part of your past might have become part of your future? In what ways did this happen for Inna?
2. Inna was committed to encourage the young soldiers on base to learn more about the German and Russian people—their varied histories, languages, and cultures. Have you had an experience when you took the time to learn more about someone else who is "not like you"? If so, how did your encounter(s) affect your thinking?

*Trust in the Lord with all your heart*
*and lean not on your own understanding;*
*in all your ways acknowledge him,*
*and he will make your paths straight.*
*(Proverbs 3:5–6, NIV)*

A Changing World

Inna's last assignment in Germany was her return to Bad Aibling and Munich. While there, she witnessed the dramatic changes around her—the rebuilding and modernization of Munich and other European cities demolished by the war. As worldwide tensions increased, there was the sharp contrast of a divided Berlin that restricted Inna's return to the city. The Wall that was created by the Soviets divided and isolated East Berlin and West Berlin. The "Iron Curtain" isolated the East from the West. The innocence of the American public was shattered by the assassination of a beloved President.

And through it all Inna realizes more changes in her life...
Where was God in all of this?

*For I know the plans I have for you, declares the Lord,*
*plans to prosper you and not to harm you,*
*plans to give you hope and a future.*
*(Jeremiah 29:11, NIV)*

# About the Author

Alice Frick Hagaman was born in Anderson, South Carolina. She grew up with her younger sister, Kathryn, and parents, Cecil and Sara Frick, in Mt. Holly and Winston-Salem, North Carolina. After graduating from Greensboro College in elementary education, Alice married the love of her life, John Hagaman. She later received a MEd degree in early childhood education from the University of North Carolina in Chapel Hill. She is currently a retired teacher in Durham, North Carolina, and enjoys providing support to educators who are pursuing National Board Certification. John and Alice have a daughter, Amy, and a son-in-law, Brent Cockerham, who have blessed them with three beautiful grandchildren; Ryan Blair, Andrew Harrison, and Shaela Elizabeth.

*Searching for Home* is Alice's first book, a completely unexpected journey that started with a Sunday morning encounter… an unforgettable moment with her friend, Inna Nichols. Alice's writing is the result of the focused times they had together when Inna poured out her deepest and most personal memories. Alice believes that the powerful connection she felt with Inna is one of the most enriching spiritual experiences of her lifetime.

CPSIA information can be obtained
at www.ICGtesting.com
Printed in the USA
BVHW090543270819
556820BV00014B/950/P